THE
Bandsaw
BOOK

THE Bandsaw BOOK

LONNIE BIRD

The Taunton Press

Front cover photo: Scott Phillips
Back cover photos: Lonnie Bird

The Taunton Press
Inspiration for hands-on living™

Text © 1999 by Lonnie Bird
Photographs © 1999 by The Taunton Press, Inc.
Illustrations © 1999 by The Taunton Press, Inc.

Printed in the United States of America
10 9 8 7 6 5 4 3

The Taunton Press, Inc., 63 South Main Street, PO Box 5506, Newtown, CT 06470-5506
e-mail: tp@taunton.com

Distributed by Publishers Group West

Library of Congress Cataloging-in-Publication Data

Bird, Lonnie.
    The bandsaw book / Lonnie Bird.
        p. cm.
    Includes bibliographical references and index.
    ISBN 1-56158-289-1
    1. Band saws. 2. Woodwork. I. Title.
    TT186.B514   1999
    684'.083—dc21   99-29603
                        CIP

About Your Safety

Working with wood is inherently dangerous. Using hand or power tools improperly or ignoring standard safety practices can lead to permanent injury or even death. Don't try to perform operations you learn about here (or elsewhere) unless you're certain they are safe for you. If something about an operation doesn't feel right, don't do it. Look for another way. We want you to enjoy the craft, so please keep safety foremost in your mind whenever you're working with wood.

Acknowledgments

I would like to thank the following people for their help with this book.

For technical assistance, I'd like to thank Torbin Helshoj of Laguna Tools, John Otto of Jet Tools, and Jeff Buske of Starrett Tools. I'd like to give special thanks to Bob Candiano of Lenox. Bob's knowledge of bandsaw blades and his willingness to help were immeasurable.

I also want to thank several people at The Taunton Press, including Helen Albert for supporting this idea, Jennifer Renjilian for her organization and encouragement, and Aimé Fraser for her patience in editing.

Additionally, I want to thank my good friend (and fellow woodworker) Jason Bennett for his help with photography. Jason was a patient stand-in for many of the photos in this book. Also, when I was busy writing, he was making many of the photo props.

Most of all, I want to thank my wife, Linda, for her patience, work, and support throughout this entire project.

Contents

Introduction

Without a doubt, the bandsaw is one of the most popular woodworking machines. In fact, surveys show that the vast majority of woodworkers own a bandsaw. Those who don't have one plan to buy one within the next year. Why is the bandsaw so popular? Certainly it must stem from the uniqueness of the saw and its application to so many areas of woodworking.

When it comes to cutting curves, the bandsaw has no equal: The narrow blade on the bandsaw can easily follow almost any contour. And the average bandsaw can cut much thicker stock than any jigsaw or scrollsaw. Yet the bandsaw can cut so much more than just curves. It also performs remarkably well while precisely cutting straight lines, such as when slicing veneer of uniform thickness or cutting intricate dovetail joints. In fact, many woodworkers would most likely be surprised to see how widely the bandsaw is used in industry for precision cutting of metal.

I wrote this book for several reasons. One was to help woodworkers explore new bandsawing techniques. Too often the bandsaw is viewed as a tool just for cutting curves. But the bandsaw, even an inexpensive one, is much more versatile than that. My aim is to help woodworkers expand their abilities by learning practical, useful methods.

I also wrote this book to provide background information so that woodworkers can understand concepts essential to using the machine. For example, the success that all of us desire from the bandsaw depends on a precisely tuned machine. The bandsaw requires careful adjustment—as much as any other woodworking machine and more than most. When you understand concepts related to adjusting the machine, you can more effectively work with it.

Additionally, I wanted to provide insight into how the bandsaw works and to help woodworkers make wise buying decisions. There are a lot of manufacturers making bandsaws these days. Many produce a great saw; others produce an average saw. And, unfortunately, some just seem to want your money. I've included information in this book to help you steer clear of the last category of manufacturers and their machines.

In the same vein, I've also included information on bandsaw blades so that woodworkers can make informed purchasing decisions about them. The blade you select will strategically affect your bandsawing success—or failure. Most consumer catalogs offer only a small selection of inexpensive carbon-steel blades, and while these blades work well for the average cut, they have major shortcomings when the cut is demanding.

Like all other woodworking tools, such as circular sawblades and router bits, bandsaw blades have become very sophisticated. If you're accustomed to using the blade that came on your bandsaw, you'll be amazed at the success you can achieve with a great blade. I've included information in this book to help you reach this level of mastery.

Finally, I wanted to combine this information in a useful, organized way. Don't just pour over this book while sitting at home—take it to your shop and get some dust between the pages! It's my hope that this book will help you achieve the success you desire with your bandsaw.

The Versatile Bandsaw

The bandsaw is one of the most useful woodworking machines you can own. It can shape flowing curves, cut precise dovetail joinery, and resaw thick boards into thin ones. With a bandsaw in your shop, you can saw graceful cabriole legs and ogee feet or even slice a small log into lumber. No other woodworking machine gives you this much versatility. And best of all, because a bandsaw blade continuously pushes the stock down on the table, a bandsaw won't kick back as a table saw might.

A bandsaw is stone simple—it is a thin, continuous ribbonlike blade turning on a set of wheels. To prevent the blade from twisting and flexing while cutting, bandsaws are equipped with guides to support the sides of the blade. A frame holds all the pieces together, and a table supports the workpiece during cutting.

The most important part of a bandsaw and the key to its versatility is the blade. Most consumer-grade bandsaws, which have a 14-in. or smaller wheel diameter, will accept blades as narrow as $\frac{1}{16}$ in. and as wide as $\frac{3}{4}$ in. Larger floor-model bandsaws, those with a wheel diameter greater than 16 in., will accept blades $1\frac{1}{4}$ in. wide or larger. This range of blade sizes is what makes the bandsaw so useful. If you mount a $\frac{1}{16}$-in. blade on your bandsaw, you can cut intricate scrolls. Change to a $\frac{3}{8}$-in. blade, and you can cut flowing, graceful curves. Change blades again to one that's $\frac{3}{4}$ in. or wider, and you're ready to slice veneer from a wide plank or saw a bowl blank for the lathe.

This chapter discusses what a bandsaw can do, how it's constructed, and what types are available. While bandsaws are simple tools, you need to understand their components and the various types before you can choose one and make the best use of its versatility.

The Bandsaw Can Do the Work of Several Tools

The bandsaw can perform the functions of a shopful of cutting tools. It can rip like a table saw, cut curves like a jigsaw, make fine cuts like a scrollsaw, saw logs like a mill, cut joints like a handsaw, and even follow templates like a router. The bandsaw also excels at two jobs that no other tool can do: cutting compound curves and resawing wide stock. Let's look at each of these functions in more detail and see what a bandsaw can do for you.

Rip like a table saw

If you've ever ripped thick hardwood stock on your table saw, you're probably aware of the problems associated with this method. The sawblade tends to bog down, sometimes stalling the motor. There may also be a lot of feed resistance, so when you're done you have burned edges on the stock. These problems occur because a table saw's blade is thick and produces a wide kerf, usually ⅛ in. It takes a lot of power to push a thick blade through heavy stock. Many table saws just don't have the horsepower to rip a thick piece of heavy hardwood.

Although it's one of the most versatile tools in any shop, the bandsaw is fairly simple. The key to its versatility is the continuous ribbonlike blade that makes it possible to cut curves, rip stock, resaw wide boards, and cut precision joints. (Photo by Scott Phillips.)

You can remedy these problems by ripping thick stock with your bandsaw. Because a bandsaw blade is so thin compared to a table-saw blade, the bandsaw quickly and easily cuts through thick maple, cherry, or any other hardwood. In technical terms, bandsaws have less feed resistance than table saws. Also, you won't have the burn

> **Waste less wood**
>
> When you must maximize the yield from a board, rip it with a bandsaw. Because the kerf is narrower, the bandsaw produces far less waste than a table saw.

marks on your stock because a bandsaw blade doesn't heat up like a table-saw blade does. Best of all, ripping with a bandsaw is safer because there is no chance of the stock being kicked back toward you as there is with a table saw (see the drawing below). The bandsaw is the safest way to rip stock that is twisted, cupped, or warped. Ripping such stock on a table saw is dangerous because the stock can bind and pinch the blade, which increases the likelihood of kickback. The constant downward pressure of the band-

Ripping thick stock on a bandsaw is safer and easier than using a table saw. Use a wide blade and a sturdy fence.

Ripping on the Bandsaw

Table saw

The spinning blade can hurl the workpiece back at the operator.

$\frac{1}{8}$-in. kerf

Force

Bandsaw

$\frac{1}{16}$-in. kerf

The blade moves downward, pushing the workpiece onto the table with no tendency to kick back.

Force

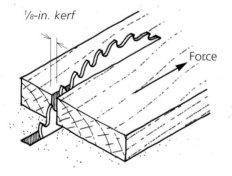

The typical ripping setup on the table-saw blade (shown at left) produces a kerf about ⅛ in. wide. It takes a lot of horsepower to remove that much material, particularly in dense hardwood or thick stock. The blade rotates toward the operator, producing a tangential force that can hurl a board back at you if not handled properly.

On the bandsaw (shown at right), the blade thickness is only ¹⁄₁₆ in. or less. There is much less material wasted in the kerf, and less horsepower is required to make the cut. The bandsaw blade pushes the stock downward onto the table and has no tendency to kick back.

saw blade pushes the stock onto the table so it can't kick back.

When ripping with my bandsaw, I use a wide, coarse blade and a fence mounted to the table to guide the stock. For details on setting up your own bandsaw for ripping, see pp. 124-126.

Cut curves like a jigsaw

For most woodworkers, the bandsaw is the tool of choice for sawing curves. No other woodworking tool performs this task as quickly or as precisely. A bandsaw's narrow blade allows you to follow the curves, while the saw's table provides support for the stock. Because the blade is continuously moving downward as you cut, the stock isn't lifted off the table as when using a jigsaw or a scrollsaw. This gives you the confidence and concentration to focus on making the cut.

When cutting curves with my bandsaw, I find it's important to use the widest possible blade that can follow the radius of the curve I'm sawing. A wide blade is easier to control and has less of a tendency to wander. I've provided a radius chart on p. 74 to help you determine which blade width to use for various kinds of cuts and more tips on sawing curves in chapter 7.

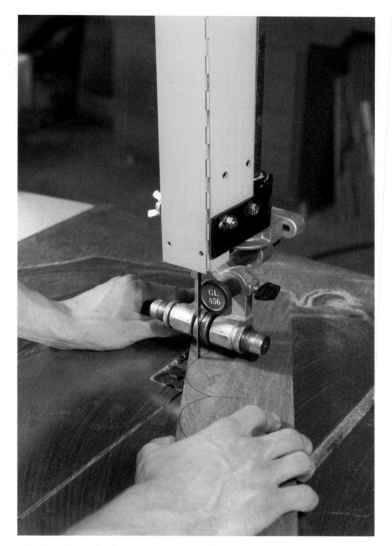

The bandsaw is the tool of choice for cutting curves. With the table's solid support and the way the blade pushes downward, you can really concentrate on following your line.

Make fine cuts like a scrollsaw

The bandsaw is also a good tool for building projects with fine, intricate scrollwork such as Chippendale-style mirrors. Blades as narrow as $1/16$ in. are available that will enable you to squeeze around the tight curves typically made on a scrollsaw (see the top photo on p. 9). In fact, I prefer a bandsaw to a scrollsaw because the scrollsaw has an annoying tendency to vibrate, and the reciprocating motion of the scrollsaw can lift the work from the table

The Bandsaw Can Handle Most Sawing Operations

I make 18th-century reproductions, and the bandsaw is indispensable to my work. I use it for everything from ripping and cutting curves to making book-matched panels and curved moldings. Here are some of the ways I used my bandsaw in the Chippendale desk shown in the photo at right.

• The gooseneck moldings on the pediment were made on the bandsaw and on the router as described in chapter 7.

• The book-matched panels in the doors were resawn on the bandsaw as described in chapter 8.

• The dividers were sawn in stacks to keep them identical as described in chapter 7.

• The drawer dovetails were cut on the bandsaw as shown in chapter 8.

• The veneers on the drawers were resawn on the bandsaw as shown in chapter 8.

• The ogee feet were cut on the bandsaw as described in chapter 7.

• The thin lumber of the dividers was resawn as described in chapter 8.

• The curved drawer fronts of the interior were roughed out on a bandsaw as described in chapter 7.

• The tenons in the door panels were made on the bandsaw as described in chapter 8.

• The arches on the tops of the doors were sawn with a special jig as shown in chapter 9.

• The arches on the tops of the panels were cut on the bandsaw as shown in chapter 7.

and spoil the cut. For more information on using narrow blades, see p. 102.

Saw logs like a lumber mill

As woodworkers, we all know how expensive lumber has become. One way to save money is to saw your own lumber on your bandsaw. Obviously, you can't saw big logs into planks for large-scale furniture, but many small logs will yield lumber that's suitable for small-scale items such as small chests, jewelry boxes, and other decorative projects.

Finding small logs suitable for sawing isn't as difficult as you might think, even if you don't live in a rural area. People who sell firewood are often willing to sell a small log or two. Better yet, many loggers and tree surgeons will give you small logs or pieces of logs for very little or nothing. Often the logs with the most spectacular figure, such as the fork or crotch of a tree, are the least desirable to professional loggers. If you saw these pieces yourself, you'll end up with some exceptionally fine lumber. If you enjoy woodturning, you'll find that the bandsaw is a great tool for sizing up small chunks of green logs for turning blanks. On pp. 164-165, I've detailed some of the things you'll need to know to turn your bandsaw into a small sawmill.

Cut joints like a handsaw

For centuries, dovetail and mortise-and-tenon joints have been the woodworker's choices for both strength and beauty. The mechanical interlock and the long grain surface area of these joints provide unparalleled strength for a wide variety

A ¹⁄₁₆-in.-wide blade makes it possible for a bandsaw to negotiate the tight curves often done on a scrollsaw.

With a proper jig, you can saw small logs on a bandsaw. This opens up the possibility of building small projects from spectacularly figured boards that might have ended up as firewood.

If your bandsaw has a tilting table, you can use it to cut precision dovetails. The bandsaw is also a good tool for cutting tenons and laps.

of woodworking applications. Dovetails are used most often to join the corners of casework and drawers, while mortise-and-tenon joints are used to make face frames for casework and paneled doors and to join legs to rails when constructing tables and chairs.

Although there are dozens of methods for making these time-honored joints, you may be surprised how quickly and precisely you can cut them with your bandsaw. Of course the process starts with the right blade for the job, and if you want to cut dovetails, your saw must have a tilting table (see the top photo at left). For more details on cutting precision joinery with your bandsaw, see pp. 146-155.

Follow templates like a router

Using a template with a woodworking machine is the fastest way to produce identical multiple parts for furniture or other woodwork. This procedure also relieves the tedium that occurs when making many identical pieces. If you own a router table, you've probably used the template-routing technique. It's very similar to the template-sawing technique. When template routing, you must first make a stiff template of plywood that is identical to the part you wish to produce. The bearing on the end of the router bit follows a template attached to the workpiece to guide the cutter along a path. Whether you're making 6 parts or 60, they all come out alike.

The same concept can be used with the bandsaw. First, clamp a notched stick to the table, positioning it around the blade, as shown in the bottom photo at left, or

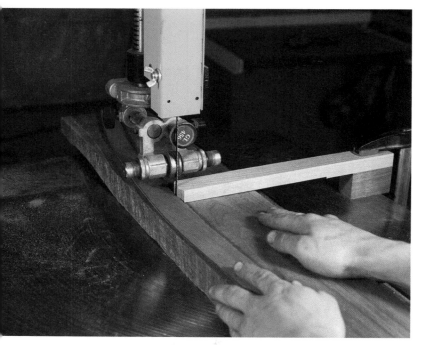

Pattern sawing on a bandsaw with a template is an efficient method for producing multiple parts. However, this method doesn't leave the workpiece with a finished edge, as would using a router with a template-cutting bit.

use a special blade that has a follower pin. Then, attach the workpiece to the template with small brads or double-sided tape. As you guide the template past the notched stick, the blade is guided through the cut to create a workpiece that is identical to the template—what you might call bandsaw cloning. Template sawing is a quick and easy way for you to make a multitude of exact copies of your original workpiece.

Although the bandsaw doesn't produce a finished surface as a router will, this technique is still much faster than laying out and sawing each piece individually. If you would like to put this technique to work on your bandsaw, see pp. 155-157.

Saw compound curves

If you enjoy building furniture with sensuous, flowing lines, then you're well aware of the bandsaw's potential in this area of woodworking. Many furniture styles, both period and contemporary, contain graceful curves that flow in two directions at once, and the bandsaw is *the* tool for creating those curves.

Once you learn to saw compound curves, you can add an extra dimension to your next furniture project. As a builder of exact reproductions of fine colonial American antiques, I use the bandsaw to create the compound curves found in cabriole legs and ogee bracket feet (see the photo above). This technique involves laying out and sawing the curves on two adjacent faces. There are some additional steps involved, such as selecting the right blade and building a stand to

The bandsaw is the only simple way to cut compound curves such as those in this cabriole leg.

support the stock, that are clearly outlined starting on p. 131.

Resaw wide panels

Resawing involves standing a board on edge and ripping it through its thickness to produce two pieces of thinner stock. You can use this technique for making matching panels by sawing a thick, oversized board into two pieces of equal thickness (see the top photo on p. 12). I like to use a figured board to produce book-matched panels, as shown in the bottom photo on p. 12, where resawn panels are mirror images of each other. Resawing is also a great way to make your own veneer out of a prized figured board. You can glue the veneer to drawer fronts for a chest so that all the fronts will match perfectly. If you need thin stock for small drawers or other small boxes, you can save lumber by resawing oversized stock rather than planing the excess thickness.

No other woodworking machine is better suited for resawing than the bandsaw. Because a bandsaw blade is thin, it

The bandsaw excels at resawing thick boards into thin ones. It's a demanding application for the saw and requires plenty of power.

creates a small kerf and therefore very little waste during sawing (see the drawing on p. 6). This means you'll get more usable stock from your expensive lumber and less sawdust. Also, the thin blade of the bandsaw creates very little feed resistance as you're sawing. If you've ever resawn with a table saw, you'll immediately notice the difference with the bandsaw.

Resawing with the bandsaw is safer too. Since the blade pushes the stock downward toward the table, there is no chance of kickback. Still another advantage is that you can resaw wider stock with your bandsaw than with a table saw. Most of the common 14-in. bandsaws can resaw a 6-in.-wide board. If you need more height capacity, you may be able to outfit your bandsaw with a riser block to extend the column to accommodate boards up to 12 in. wide. But if you plan to do a lot of resawing, a large-capacity floor-model bandsaw is your best option. It will have the motor, frame, wheels, and guides to handle the wider blades and the greater blade tension needed for successful resawing. For a detailed description of resawing, see pp. 141-145.

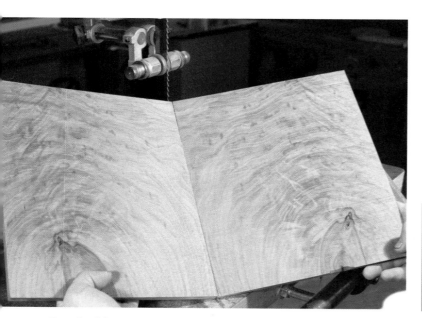

Two freshly resawn boards opened like a book are mirror images of each other. Book-matched boards such as these can add distinction to your next project.

How much power?

If you plan to do a lot of resawing with your bandsaw, you'll need a machine with at least a 1-hp motor. A motor with 2 hp or 3 hp is even better.

Bandsaw Anatomy

Bandsaws are unique among woodworking machines. Most other saws, such as table saws, radial-arm saws, and chopsaws, use a somewhat thick circular blade. A circular sawblade must be stiff for mounting on the machine's shaft or arbor. But a bandsaw blade can be made thin and flexible because most of the stiffness is gained as it is tensioned around the wheels of the saw. However, a flexible blade requires a system of wheels, tires, and guides to support it and a strong frame to support the wheels and maintain blade tension.

In this section, I'll briefly describe each of the bandsaw's major components (see the drawing on p. 14). In chapter 2, I'll go into more detail, including variations, options, and aftermarket additions.

Frame

The most important component of every bandsaw is the frame. The frame supports the wheels, table, and guides, and it must be rigid enough to resist bending under the load of a tensioned blade. Years ago, all bandsaw frames were cast iron. Even though cast iron is still a good choice for frame material, it's expensive to manufacture. Many frames are now made of steel or aluminum.

The lower frame has a column to one side that supports the upper wheel. This wheel-support column may be an integral part of the frame, or on cast frames it may be a separate piece that's bolted on. If the column is bolted on, you can typically add a riser block to increase the cutting height of the saw.

Wheels

Most bandsaws have two wheels, although some have three. The upper wheel adjusts vertically to provide blade tension or to release tension for blade changes. It also has an adjustment that angles the wheel to keep the sawblade tracking properly. The motor powers the lower wheel, either directly or by a V-belt and pulley system.

Bandsaw wheels are typically made of cast iron, although some manufacturers cast their wheels from aluminum to keep costs down. Although I prefer iron wheels for their weight, aluminum wheels can work well if they are balanced.

Tires

All bandsaws have rubber tires stretched around their wheels. The tires give the blade traction and cushion the blade to protect the teeth. Most bandsaw tires are crowned, meaning that they are higher in the middle and slope toward the edges. This makes it easier to keep the blade running on track. The tires are an important part of keeping a bandsaw running smoothly. Many bandsaw problems can be traced to worn tires.

Motor

Bandsaw motors range in size from $\frac{1}{3}$ hp on some benchtop saws to 10 hp on the largest industrial saws. Generally, the larger the motor, the better. Most 12-in. to 14-in. consumer-grade saws come with

The Parts of a Bandsaw

This is the prototypical 14-in. bandsaw made by Delta. Many other companies make similar saws.

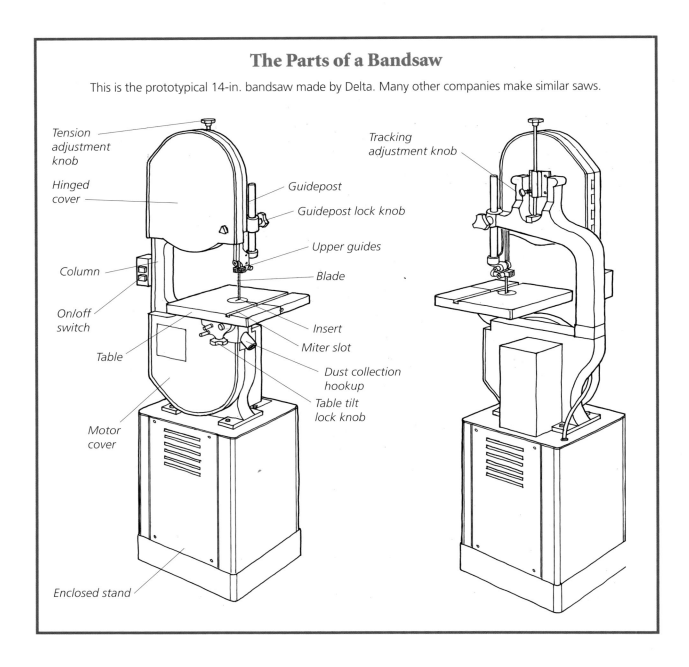

Tension adjustment knob

Hinged cover

Column

On/off switch

Table

Motor cover

Enclosed stand

Tracking adjustment knob

Guidepost

Guidepost lock knob

Upper guides

Blade

Insert

Miter slot

Dust collection hookup

Table tilt lock knob

a ½-hp motor. A motor of ¾ hp or 1 hp is better for a saw this size, especially if you want to resaw.

Blades

Bandsaw blades consist of a thin, flexible steel ribbon that is made continuous by welding the ends together. Teeth are milled onto one edge of the steel band, and some blades have hard steel alloy or carbide teeth that are brazed onto the band to provide extra resistance to wear. Like all woodworking sawblades and cutterheads, bandsaw blades have become very sophisticated in their design. The importance of using a quality blade can't be overstated. For a detailed discussion on choosing blades, see chapter 4.

Guides

Bandsaws have two sets of guides to keep the blade from twisting or flexing during cutting. Each guide supports the blade from both sides and from the back so that the blade won't be pushed off the wheels during cutting (see the drawing at right). The blade runs in between the fixed blocks or bearings on the guide. The lower guide is fixed below the table, while the upper guide is attached to a sliding post that allows the guide to be adjusted vertically to accommodate stock of varying thicknesses. There are several guide designs, but all guides use either friction blocks or bearings to provide the actual support. For more information on the types of guides, see pp. 27-31. For suggestions on choosing guides, see p. 48.

Table

The table on a bandsaw provides a rigid, stable surface for support of the stock as it is being cut. Most bandsaw tables are made of cast iron for its strength and weight. The table is supported by trunnions, which are curved arms that allow the table to tilt for making angled cuts (see the bottom photo on p. 34). Tables are typically square and approximately the size of the wheel diameter. Because the table is centered on the blade, there is a gap between the table and the column. Most large bandsaws have an extension table to fill that gap. Many tables have a slot parallel to the blade for using a miter gauge or jigs.

Fence

The fence provides a fixed distance from the blade when making precise cuts to a specific size, such as when ripping or cutting joinery. It also provides critical support when resawing. The bandsaw fence must be rigid and lock firmly to the table.

Typical Bandsaw Guides

Guides support the blade to prevent both side-to-side and backward motion. This drawing shows guide blocks, which are standard equipment on most midsize bandsaws.

Blade — Guidepost — Thrust bearing — Upper guide assembly — Guide block — Guide holder — Workpiece — Table — Thrust bearing — Guide block — Lower guide assembly — Guide holder

Supporting narrow blades

When using a narrow blade, make a set of hardwood guide blocks and adjust them to completely surround the blade. The blade's teeth won't be damaged, and your blade will have maximum support for intricate cuts.

Types of Bandsaws

Bandsaws are sized according to throat capacity, which is the distance from the blade to the column. On a two-wheel bandsaw, the throat is always less than the wheel diameter. Three-wheel bandsaws have larger throats because their wheels form a triangle.

Because the bandsaw is so simple, almost every manufacturer of woodworking machines makes one. As you might expect, designs vary considerably and there is a wide range of bandsaws to choose from.

> **Adding resaw capacity**
>
> Most 14-in. saws can be expanded to greater throat capacity by adding a riser block.

Even so, bandsaws fall into four basic categories: floor models, saws that are mounted on a stand, small benchtop models, and special resaw bandsaws.

When it comes to bandsaws, bigger is better. A big saw can typically handle narrow blades and make small, intricate cuts, but a small saw can't handle wide blades and resaw wide boards or reach to the center of a wide panel. Also, blade breakage is less of a problem on large saws; the small-diameter wheels on little bandsaws put more stress on a blade.

Large saws have further advantages over their smaller cousins. Large saws are heavier and are often (but not always) better balanced, so there is less vibration to spoil the cut. Next, I'll discuss the pros and cons of various designs.

Big floor-model saws like this one are real workhorses. They have the size and power to handle the big jobs but can also be fitted with narrow blades to make delicate cuts.

Floor models

Among bandsaws, floor models are the real workhorses. They have the size and power needed for the heaviest cuts. The largest industrial bandsaws have wheel diameters of 42 in. and a broad table like the top of an aircraft carrier. These heavy-duty machines are incredibly smooth running and have the power to slice their way through the densest hardwoods. Okay, so you really don't need that much bandsaw—most of us don't. But don't overlook the European steel-frame floor-model bandsaws in the 18-in. to 24-in. range. They have plenty of power and capacity, smooth performance, and the smaller ones can be had at a price that's not much beyond some of the most expensive 14-in. saws.

If you're serious about wanting a big floor-model saw but your budget is limited, you may want to check out an older machine. Many old but good cast-iron bandsaws can be bought for bargain-basement prices. These saws were made at the time when woodworking machinery manufacturers used iron—and plenty of it. However, there are potential problems. It may be expensive or impossible to buy parts for an old machine, although universal items such as guides and tires are available for virtually any bandsaw (see Sources on pp. 196-197). Most old industrial bandsaws have three-phase motors. Sometimes a three-phase motor can be swapped for a single-phase motor of equal horsepower, but more often the motors are direct drive and can't be readily replaced because of their special mounting brackets. So if you're searching for an old cast-iron bandsaw, be prepared to spend a few hundred dollars extra for a phase converter.

A 14-in. bandsaw like this one is inexpensive and versatile. It is the corner-stone of many home and small professional shops.

Stand models

Every woodworker is familiar with the multitude of 14-in. bandsaws on the market. These midsize bandsaws, with a wheel diameter of 12 in. to 16 in., are extremely popular. These saws are the VW Beetles of woodworking. They're small and inexpensive yet they usually get you where you're going. Their moderate price tag makes them especially appealing, and their size is adequate for most woodworking applications. My 14-in. bandsaw served me well for many years.

Because of their small stature, saws of this type are mounted on steel legs or on a sheet-metal cabinet to raise the table to a comfortable working height. The stand also provides a place to mount the motor. Most saws in this category have about 6 in. of resaw capacity, but adding a riser block can typically double that.

Although most stand-model saws are sturdily built, the materials and workmanship are not always the best. Many have vibration problems that can be blamed on inexpensive die-cast pulleys, out-of-balance wheels, and lumpy tires. Although you may be able to correct these problems yourself (I'll explain how in chapter 6), for a few hundred dollars more you can get a smooth-running bandsaw right out of the box. I would suppose that most woodworkers wouldn't buy a new truck that was considered a

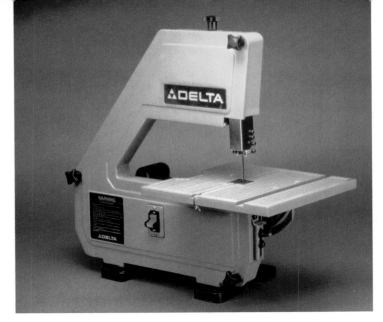

Although not designed for heavy cutting, a small benchtop saw is ideal for small projects. (Photo courtesy Delta.)

three wheels that form a triangular-shaped frame to give more room between the blade and the column. This is the only advantage of a three-wheeled bandsaw.

Three-wheelers often have difficulty tracking blades, they lack frame stiffness, and their small-diameter wheels are prone to breaking blades. I speak from unfortunate experience with a three-wheeled saw. My first bandsaw was a 1950s three-wheeler, and although it was a sturdy machine, I soon discovered the many disadvantages of this type of saw. Most manufacturers have abandoned this problem-plagued design. The only three-wheeled bandsaws I've seen recently are the lightweight benchtop models.

Due to their size and power limitations, benchtop saws are not designed for heavy cutting. But if you're interested in small craft projects and your shop space or budget is limited, one of these inexpensive little saws might fit your needs.

Blade strength

Three-wheel bandsaws have relatively small wheels, so they require thinner, more flexible blades than saws with larger-diameter wheels.

---

kit—one that needed balancing and tuning before driving. Why buy a bandsaw that needs work before making the first cut? There are several manufacturers, both foreign and domestic, that make great 14-in. bandsaws. For more information on what to look for in a new saw, see chapter 3.

Benchtop bandsaws

The popularity of woodworking as a hobby has caused a market explosion of small benchtop machines, including bandsaws. These little saws can be found in almost any woodworking tool catalog, home improvement center, or discount department store.

Benchtop saws typically have 8-in. or 10-in. wheels and a one-piece die-cast aluminum frame. Some benchtop saws have

Resaw bandsaws

Resaw machines are specially equipped with 2-in.- or 3-in.-wide blades. They are designed to handle the high tension required to get maximum performance from such wide blades. Resaw bandsaws do one thing really well: resaw wide planks. They can be fitted with a narrow blade for cutting curves, but doing so requires changing the guides. For most shops, the resaw bandsaw will be the second or even third bandsaw. They have become especially popular in small custom furniture shops. If you're continually resawing thick boards or you enjoy making your own veneer, this may be the saw for you.

Bandsaw Features and Options

Before you buy or use a bandsaw, it's helpful to understand how the machine is put together. Knowing what makes a bandsaw work will make it easier for you to undertake small repairs and give your saw the occasional tweaking it needs to keep it running smoothly. And if you haven't yet bought a saw, knowing what features and options are available will prepare you to make a wise purchase.

Frames

The most important part of any bandsaw is the frame. It supports all the major components of the machine, including the wheels, table, guides, and sometimes the motor. The frame must be rigid enough to resist flexing or bending when the blade is fully tensioned. If the frame is not rigid, it will be impossible to get the blade tight enough to do some operations such as resawing. If you plan to do a lot of resawing, you'll especially appreciate a rigid frame. Although bandsaw designs vary widely, there are essentially only three types of frames: two-piece cast iron, one-piece cast iron (or sometimes aluminum), and the welded steel box.

Cast-iron frames

For more than a hundred years, manufacturers have used cast iron for bandsaw frames and for good reason. Cast iron is strong enough to handle the stress from a fully tensioned blade, and it's great at absorbing vibration. If you've ever stepped up to an old 36-in. Tannewitz bandsaw while it's running, then you already know what I'm talking about (see

19

Weighing well over a ton, this 36-in. Tannewitz industrial bandsaw has a cast-iron frame that's rigid enough to tension wide blades and heavy enough to dampen vibration.

the photo above). The machine's massive, curved gooseneck frame rises gracefully from the base to provide rigid support for even the widest blades. This iron giant weighs a ton and a half, enough to dampen any vibration from the drivetrain or blade. In contrast, a lightweight bandsaw may vibrate so badly that you'll have difficulty following your layout line.

But you don't have to buy an industrial saw to get a cast-iron frame. Many of today's consumer-grade saws also have iron frames. The frame is typically cast in two pieces—a base supporting the table, lower wheel, and lower guides, and a column supporting the upper wheel and upper guides. The two castings fasten together at the base of the column. This two-piece frame design allows you to easily increase the saw's cutting height by adding an accessory extension block, which is bolted in the column between the two pieces. The extension block raises the guidepost height by about 6 in. When you buy the block, you also get longer guards and an extended guidepost to support the upper guide. Keep in mind that you'll have to buy longer blades and you may need to buy a motor with more horsepower.

There is another kind of cast-iron frame used primarily on inexpensive bandsaws. Some manufacturers use this design for saws in the 14-in. to 16-in. range, but most saws of this type are smaller and sometimes cast in aluminum. The frame and wheel covers are cast to form a one-piece structure. To achieve rigidity, the casting is heavily ribbed (see the photo at right on the facing page). This design isn't used on large floor-model bandsaws because it just isn't rigid enough for heavy resawing. Because most bandsaws of this type lack the power and capacity for all but the smallest work, many woodworkers who buy a small benchtop saw of this design soon outgrow its limited capabilities.

Even though having a cast-iron frame has definite advantages, it isn't an ironclad guarantee of a smooth-running saw. Nor

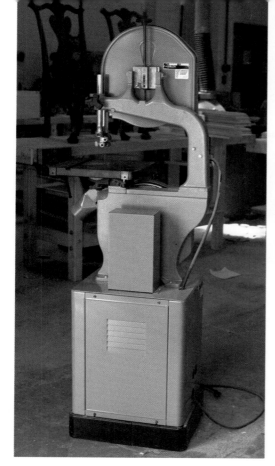

The joint between the two parts of the cast-iron frame of this 14-in. bandsaw is just below the level of the table. A riser block can be bolted between the two pieces to double the resaw height.

Many smaller bandsaws use a one-piece cast frame. This aluminum frame has ribs cast into it to increase strength and stiffness.

is cast iron really necessary. A strong, rigid bandsaw can be made using sheet steel folded and welded to make a box-type frame.

Steel box frames

In the long history of the bandsaw, the idea of using a steel frame is a relatively new one. But the idea has caught on, as steel-frame bandsaws are steadily gaining popularity among woodworkers. To make a steel frame, manufacturers fold and weld sheets of heavy-gauge steel to make a rigid box. A steel-frame bandsaw is considerably less expensive to build than a cast-iron bandsaw of the same size. As a result, many woodworkers are discovering that they can afford the large bandsaw they've always wanted.

Cast iron is excellent at absorbing vibration, while steel transmits energy rather than absorbing it. So how do manufacturers make steel-frame saws that run smoothly? The key is balance. To run

A bandsaw with a welded steel frame, like this European-made model, is stiff and strong as well as being lightweight and moderately priced. Note the plywood platform to bring the table height to a comfortable level.

vibration-free, all of the rotating parts (the wheels and pulleys) are extremely well balanced. There are other items that factor into the balancing equation, such as motors, tires, and V-belts. But the bottom line is that manufacturing has dramatically improved since the days when all bandsaw frames were huge and cast from iron. Today, expensive cast iron is not necessary as long as vibration is kept to a minimum.

Wheels and Covers

The blade on a bandsaw wraps around two (or sometimes three) wheels that are mounted to the frame and hidden behind hinged covers. The wheels keep the blade in tension and transmit the turning power from the motor to the blade. The upper wheel adjusts vertically to tension the blade or to release tension when changing blades. There is also an adjustment to tilt the upper wheel slightly to get the blade tracking on the center of the wheel.

Wheels

As a rule, blades last longer on saws that have large wheel diameters. This is because a blade and its weld are flexed around the wheels several hundred times each minute when the saw is running. This continuous flexing places a great deal of stress on a sawblade. Naturally, blades break more often when they are flexed tightly around small-diameter wheels. Manufacturers of small bandsaws overcome this problem by outfitting their saws with thin blades. However, thin blades flex

---

Wheel diameter and blades

Many manufacturers recommend that their blades not be used on wheels with diameters of less than 12 in. The greater the wheel diameter, the less likely the blade is to get brittle and work-hardened by the severe flexing it undergoes as it spins around a small-diameter wheel.

Bandsaw wheels cast from aluminum perform well when properly balanced.

Cast-iron wheels have a slight advantage over aluminum wheels. The weight of a cast-iron wheel creates a flywheel effect, and the added inertia helps to propel the blade through the wood.

and twist excessively during contour cutting, which makes it difficult or impossible to accurately follow a layout line.

Another concern with bandsaw wheels is balance. Dynamic balancing of the wheels is a major factor in smooth performance. This involves balancing the wheels as they are spinning by using a machine similar to those used to balance automobile tires. Some manufacturers of lower-cost bandsaws use static balancing, which is not as precise. Still others don't bother balancing the wheels at all. It's no wonder that some bandsaws vibrate so wildly.

Tires

All bandsaw wheels have rubber or plastic tires to cushion the blade and give it traction. Tires mount to the wheels in one of

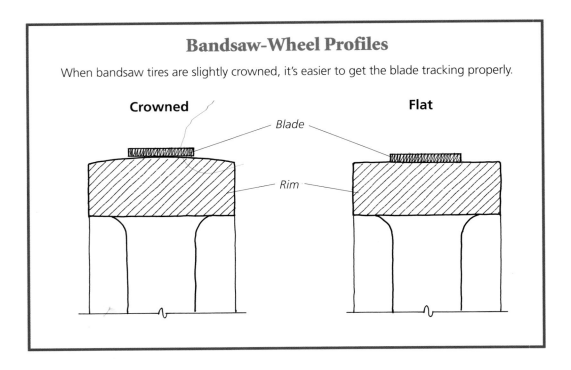

Bandsaw-Wheel Profiles

When bandsaw tires are slightly crowned, it's easier to get the blade tracking properly.

Crowned

Flat

Blade

Rim

Fixing vibration

If your bandsaw suddenly develops a vibration, the first thing to do is to check the tires for dirt, pitch, cracks, or missing pieces.

---

three ways: They are stretched onto the wheel, glued onto the wheel, or they snap and lock into a groove in the wheel's perimeter. The snap-on type is the easiest to replace.

To make it easier to keep the blade tracking properly, most bandsaw tires are slightly crowned. This means the middle of the tire's surface is slightly higher than the edges (see the drawing above). On a

crowned tire, the blade naturally tends to ride toward the tire's center.

Although most bandsaw tires are crowned, some are flat, particularly those on saws 18 in. and larger. The theory is that flat tires give more support to blades that are more than ¾ in. wide. In practice, I believe it's easier to keep blades tracking on a crowned tire. The crown only needs to be very slight, so wide blades can still have the support that they need.

Just like the tires on your car, bandsaw tires become worn with age and use. And like your car's tires, worn bandsaw tires can create a lot of problems. Narrow blades cut grooves in the tires, and this can make it difficult or impossible to keep the blade tracking. As tires age they crack, and the cracks can cause the blade to vibrate. Cracks can become so bad that chunks of the tire come loose and fly off as the wheel turns. As you might imagine, this can cause the blade to bounce and vibrate wildly.

Sawdust can build up on your bandsaw's tires and cause problems similar to those created by wear. Surprisingly, even a small amount of sawdust buildup can cause problems. Some manufacturers solve this dilemma by mounting a brush that rubs against the lower wheel (see the photo at right). If your saw doesn't have a brush, you can easily install one yourself. A portion of a stiff-bristle scrub brush works well, and it can be attached to a bracket so it contacts the lower tire.

A brush works wonders to keep sawdust from building up on the tires. This one was part of the original equipment, but you can make your own from a stiff scrub brush mounted on a piece of angle iron.

Wheel covers

It's hard to imagine, but the earliest bandsaws had no covers over the wheels and blade. With so many feet of exposed blade, a wrong move could be disastrous—not to mention what could happen if a blade broke or came off of the wheels. Covers on a bandsaw are vital for your safety, and thankfully all contemporary bandsaws have covers to shield you from the turning wheels and moving blade.

Changing a blade requires removing the covers, so to make the process fast and hassle-free, the covers should be hinged and equipped with a quick-release catch. Twenty years ago, many consumer-grade

> **Keep tires clean**
> Even if your saw has a brush to scrub away the sawdust, the tires will still benefit from an occasional cleaning.

bandsaws had unhinged covers. Both top and bottom covers had to be removed to change the blade, and each one was secured by two screws. Since I owned a saw like that, I can say that having unhinged covers made blade changing slow and annoying. Unfortunately, some manufacturers still design covers this way.

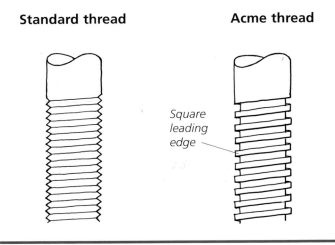
Tension Screws and Gauges

The tension screw on a bandsaw is used to move the upper wheel up or down to tension the blade. Although the tension screw is a simple device, I've seen plenty of problems with inadequate screws. The most common is stripped threads, which are not rare when tension screws are made with standard machine-screw-type threads.

It's better to use Acme-style threads for the tension screw because they can handle more load (see the drawing at left). This is the same style of thread that's found on pipe clamps. Acme threads have a square leading edge rather than a sharp leading edge as do ordinary machine-screw threads. Acme threads are more expensive to manufacture so they are typically found only on premium bandsaws.

The tension screw is turned by a hand-wheel that is located either above or just below the upper wheel. I prefer to have the handwheel located below the wheel because it's easier to reach. I also prefer a

A large, easy-to-grip tensioning wheel makes it easy to crank up the tension on a wide blade.

Tires and tension

To prolong the life of your bandsaw's tires, release the blade tension at the end of the day. Leaving the saw tensioned for days or weeks can leave permanent ridges in the tires. Prolonged tension can even distort wheels and cause bearings to fail prematurely.

large handwheel with spokes so I can get a firm grip while adjusting the blade tension. I've used some bandsaws with small, smooth handwheels that are difficult to grip.

Almost every new bandsaw has a tension gauge that is supposed to tell how much tension is on the blade. The problem is that most are inaccurate at best and many are way off. Use them only as a rough guide to blade tension.

Guides

Bandsaw guides support the blade and limit side-to-side and backward movement. All bandsaws have guides mounted both above and below the table (see the photos below). Each guide has three support members: one on each side of the blade to prevent lateral flexing and one behind the blade to prevent the feed pressure from pushing the blade off the

---

Guide position
For maximum blade support, the lower guides should be as close to the underside of the table as possible.

The lower guides are fixed in place beneath the table to provide support as the blade exits the stock. These lower guides are mounted several inches below the table; on some saws the lower guides are much closer to the underside of the table.

The upper guides are mounted on a sliding post that adjusts up and down to accommodate different thicknesses of lumber.

Steel blocks are standard on most midsize bandsaws.

groove machined into the edge of the bearing. This is an effective design that is typically found on the guides of heavy industrial saws.

Block guides

Stationary blocks are the most common type of guide. They're used on both industrial and consumer bandsaws. Blocks are popular with bandsaw manufacturers because they are simple and inexpensive. But that doesn't mean that they're inferior or ineffective. In fact, guide blocks provide excellent blade support, especially when cutting curves. This is because they have a broader contact area than bearing guides. Additionally, because of their square shape, guide blocks provide their support closer to the stock, where the cut is actually made. I've tried both block- and bearing-type guides on my bandsaw, and while bearings do have their advantages, I prefer the blocks for contour cutting because of the superior blade support that they provide.

However, there are some disadvantages to blocks. For one, they need periodic maintenance. Friction between the blade and the block wears grooves or steps in the block faces, which limit their effectiveness. This can easily be corrected by occasionally removing the blocks from the guide and truing the block face with a file. Eventually, the blocks end up too short for the setscrew to hold so you'll have to replace them. Another disadvantage is that if steel blocks are adjusted incorrectly and the teeth come in contact with the blade, the blade will be irreparably damaged.

wheels. The side supports can be either bearings, which spin when they come in contact with the blade, or stationary steel blocks, sometimes called jaw blocks (see the photo above).

The rear support is called a thrust wheel, which spins as it makes contact with the moving blade. Some thrust wheels are simply a bearing positioned so that the blade contacts the outer edge of the bearing's face. Although this method provides excellent blade support, the face of the bearing eventually becomes worn and the bearing must be replaced. The best thrust-bearing design is one in which a hardened steel disk or wheel is pressed over the face of the bearing where it contacts the blade.

Still another style of thrust wheel is one in which the bearing is positioned so that the blade contacts the edge of the bearing rather than the face. The blade sits in a

The Truth about Steel Guide Blocks

There has been a lot of misinformation lately about the damage that steel guide blocks inflict on bandsaw blades. Here's the theory: The heat generated by the friction between the steel blocks and the blade shortens the life of the blade by either causing the teeth to lose their temper (which makes them dull rapidly) or by weakening the blade until it breaks. The theory also holds that you must replace steel blocks with plastic or composite blocks.

The theory sounds good, but in reality there isn't enough heat generated by friction with the guide blocks to have any effect on the blade. Blades get hot during cutting, but the heat is generated at the tooth tip, not from the guide blocks. Besides, the heat is only a problem when resawing with a carbon-steel blade. Bimetal and carbide-tipped blades can withstand much more heat at the tooth tip, which is one reason why they are better suited for resawing.

Likewise, the small amount of friction with the guides has no effect whatsoever on the breaking of blades. Blades break when they become work-hardened from flexing around the saw's wheels hundreds of times each minute the saw is running. The guides have nothing to do with it.

Do plastic or composite guide blocks have any advantages over steel guide blocks? Yes. They won't dull the teeth if the blade accidentally comes in contact with them. And when using tiny $1/16$-in. scrolling blades, it's best to surround the blade with the blocks for maximum support. But blocks of scrap hardwood work as well as those made of plastic or composite—and best of all, they're free.

Plastic or composite guide blocks wear very quickly and need frequent adjustment and replacement. If you want longer blade life, I recommend you spend your money on better blades.

Cool Blocks You can replace the steel blocks with "Cool Blocks," a brand name for a guide block made from a fibrous material that has been impregnated with a dry lubricant. Cool Blocks make it possible to run tiny $1/16$-in. blades on your saw. Since the soft material will not damage blade teeth, you can locate the blocks so that the blade is completely sandwiched between the blocks. Using a $1/16$-in. blade and having the guides adjusted in that way, you can cut incredibly tight turns with your bandsaw—the kind of cuts normally made on a scrollsaw.

Aftermarket blocks are easier to adjust and offer more surface area than steel blocks.

Shopmade hardwood guide blocks support very narrow blades without damaging a blade's teeth.

Hardwood guide blocks You can also replace the steel blocks with hardwood blocks (see the top photo at left). I use a dense, tight-grain wood such as maple. To make the guide blocks, I cut narrow strips of hardwood to fit the guides on my saw, then cut the strip into short pieces. I always make several sets of blocks because they wear out so quickly. When they get worn, I simply toss them out and install a new pair.

Bearing guides

Bearing guides, sometimes called roller guides, look similar to block guides except that they use bearings to support the sides of the blade. There are two distinct styles of bearing guides: American and European.

Bearing guides rotate as the blade turns, which reduces friction. American-style bearing guides contact the blade with the perimeter of the guide.

American-style bearings If you've purchased a recent American-made industrial bandsaw, it probably has bearing guides (see the bottom photo at left). You can also purchase aftermarket bearing guides and install them yourself on most popular saws (see Sources on pp. 196-197). Bearing guides use three bearings to support the sawblade. Just as with block guides, a thrust bearing is mounted behind the blade to prevent feed pressure from pushing the blade off the wheels, but this style has two more bearings mounted on either side of the blade for lateral support. Each bearing spins as the blade makes contact, so there is very little friction between the blade and the guide.

European-style bearings In recent years, steel-frame bandsaws imported from Italy have steadily gained in popularity among professional woodworkers and serious hobbyists. These sturdy, smooth-running bandsaws are economical, especially in sizes larger than 14 in. If you've seen these bandsaws in advertisements or in woodworking shows, you've probably noticed their unusual-looking guides (see the photo at right). They have bearings on three sides to support the blade as American-style bearing guides do, but the side bearings are mounted so that the blade contacts the face of the bearing rather than the edge.

As another advantage, European guides have thumbwheels and knurled locking rings for easy adjustments. You don't have to search for tools to adjust these guides. The side bearings have a micrometer-type adjustment with a locking ring to hold the bearing in position. Unfortunately, the thrust bearing doesn't have a micrometer adjustment, but it does have a locking wing nut so you won't have to search for an Allen wrench.

As a disadvantage, European guides are large and take up a lot of space. This isn't a problem on the top guide, which is mounted to the guidepost, but the lower guide is too large to fit under the table. It ends up mounted in the lower cabinet, several inches below the table. Although this arrangement works, I sometimes miss the additional support provided by having the guide directly beneath the table, especially when I'm turning the workpiece through an intricate series of tight turns.

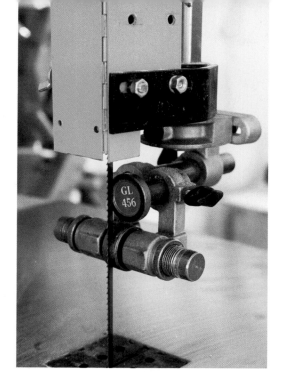

European-style bearing guides contact the blade on their faces and provide a larger bearing surface. They can be adjusted without a wrench and can be lowered closer to the cut than American-style bearing guides.

Installing guides

Before I install hardwood block guides to support narrow blades, I cut a small notch into one of the blocks and position the blade into the notch. This extra support prevents the tiny blade from twisting in the cut.

Guideposts

Mounted to the frame of a bandsaw, a guidepost adjusts the vertical height of the upper guides to compensate for different thicknesses of stock. A sheet-metal guard is attached to the guidepost to shroud the moving blade and prevent accidental contact.

The single most important aspect of a guidepost is its rigidity. If the guidepost deflects, the quality of the cut will be affected. If the deflection problem can be

Typically found on large, premium-quality bandsaws, this sturdy guidepost has a rack-and-pinion system for easy adjustments.

traced to a loose bracket or fastener, then the problem is easily corrected. But when the guidepost is securely locked in the bandsaw's frame and it continues to deflect, it's a sign that the guidepost material lacks sufficient stiffness for the job.

Also important to guidepost design is the squareness of the post to the table. If both the front and side of the post are not 90° to the saw table, you'll have to readjust the guides each time you change the height of the guidepost. This is a real nuisance, and I wouldn't buy any saw with this problem.

The best guidepost designs—those with the greatest rigidity—use a square, round, or octagonal post machined from a bar of steel. If the saw frame is made of cast iron, a hole is machined into the casting to accept the post. If the bandsaw frame is fabricated from steel, bushings are typically welded into the frame as a fitting for the guidepost.

Some smaller bandsaws use heavy-gauge sheet metal for the guidepost. The metal is folded to form an L-shape to give it rigidity. Although not as expensive as a solid-steel post, this design seems to be adequate for the smaller bandsaws on which it's used.

The combined weight of the guidepost, guide, and guard can be substantial, especially on large saws. When you loosen the screw that locks the guidepost, you'll have to support the guidepost assembly to keep it from suddenly crashing down onto the table. On better-quality bandsaws, this problem may be solved in one of several ways.

First, some machines have a counterweight to balance the weight of the guidepost assembly. A steel cable in the saw's column suspends the counterweight. The cable is wrapped around pulleys to keep it moving smoothly through the saw's frame as the guidepost is raised or lowered. The system is reminiscent of an old-style window sash that uses weights suspended inside the window frame. I've used a bandsaw with this design for a number of years, and it's a good system. It makes raising and lowering a heavy guidepost smooth and effortless.

Another system for supporting and adjusting the guidepost is the rack and pinion. Machined into the guidepost are gear teeth, which engage a small gear inside the saw cabinet (see the photo above). The small gear is fastened to a knob or handwheel on the outside of the cabinet. This is an excellent design that makes guidepost adjustments easy as well as precise.

Small saws with stamped-steel guide-posts typically have a friction device to prevent the guideposts from dropping suddenly during adjustments (see the photo at right). Although this design serves its purpose, guidepost adjustments seem stiff and awkward compared to the counterweight or rack-and-pinion designs.

Tables

The purpose of a bandsaw table is obvi-ous: It supports the stock as it is being cut. But some bandsaw tables do this simple job better than others. A good-quality table is one that's made from cast iron that has been machined flat. If you plan to saw thick, heavy stock, the table should be able to support the work with-out flexing. To maximize strength and stiffness, many tables are heavily ribbed.

To allow for blade changes, a table has a slot that runs from the throat to the table edge, either at the front or right side. Placing the slot to the side allows the trunnions to be spaced farther apart, which makes the table stiffer. To keep the table halves aligned at the blade slot, a tapered pin is inserted into a hole in the table edge. If the blade slot is in the front edge of the table, a fence rail may be used instead of a pin.

If a table is warped, the two halves will suddenly twist out of alignment when the pin or rail is removed. A small amount of misalignment shouldn't be a concern, but a saw with a severely warped table is not usable.

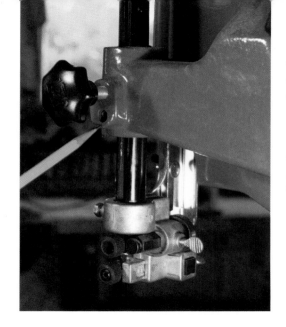

This simple friction device, found on a 14-in. bandsaw, uses a spring-loaded bearing to prevent the guidepost from falling.

The larger a saw's table, the more use-ful it will be. It's difficult to saw long, curved workpieces such as a cabriole leg when one end keeps dropping off the table. Most tables are square, the length of each side roughly equivalent to the wheel diameter of the saw. Therefore, a 14-in. saw has a table that measures about 14 in. by 14 in. A 36-in. bandsaw has a large table that rivals those found on table saws.

The table is centered on the blade, so it doesn't completely fill the space between the blade and the saw's column (called the throat). On some saws, an iron or sheet-metal auxiliary table is bolted onto the main table to fill this void. This is a nice feature, and the added support is appreci-ated when sawing large workpieces.

Don't overlook the height of the saw table from the floor. In the United States, the standard height seems to be around 40 in. to 42 in. However, European band-saws can be quite low in height, some having tables only 35 in. high. Bending over a table that low for long periods of time may give you back pain and stiffness. To increase the short stature of my saw, I built a simple plywood box as a stand and filled it with sand to make the saw more stable.

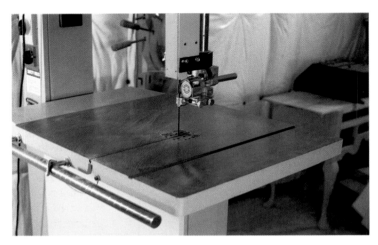

The large table on this bandsaw provides ample support for the workpiece. Note the auxiliary table that fills up the area between the table and the frame.

Trunnions bolted to the underside of the saw table allow it to tilt for cutting angles. (Photo by Scott Phillips.)

Trunnions

The table is fastened to curved supports called trunnions that allow the table to tilt for cutting angles (see the bottom photo at left). For strength, the trunnions should be made of cast iron, although some are die-cast or stamped steel. To stiffen the table, the trunnions should be spaced as far apart as possible.

Although I don't recall ever seeing a bandsaw with a nontilting table, some tables tilt farther than others. There's plenty of room for tilting to the right (as you stand facing the teeth), so tables can typically tilt 45° in that direction. However, the frame of the saw limits the angle of the tilt to the left. Although most bandsaw tables can tilt 5° to the left, some can tilt as much as 15°. In most cases, an adjustable stop is provided that enables you to quickly return the table to 90°.

Inserts

Where the blade passes through the center of the table, there is a large hole to prevent the blade and the table from damaging each other no matter what the table angle. An insert of aluminum or plastic is set into the table to fill the space around the blade. For maximum support of the workpiece at the cut, the insert should be flush to the table.

Miter slots

Most bandsaw tables have a slot for a miter gauge. The slot can be a nuisance because it sometimes catches the workpiece, so you may want to fill the slot with a strip of wood. A hard, dense wood like maple works best. Make the strip to fit snugly, then simply press it into place. You can easily remove it if you want to use the slot for a jig.

The standard miter-slot size in the United States is ⅜ in. by ¾ in. This means that you can use a miter gauge from one of your other machines. European saws typically have a smaller slot, which means you'll have to order an accessory miter gauge from the dealer.

Fences

A fence is invaluable for ripping, resawing, and cutting precision joinery. A good fence should lock firmly in any position to a track or rail on the edges of a table, and it should have sufficient stiffness to resist deflecting under sideward pressure. The best fences are cast iron or extruded aluminum. I'd avoid folded sheet-metal fences. Some fences have an adjustment to compensate for drift.

Motors and Drivetrains

I remember the 36-in. bandsaw in the first shop where I worked. I was impressed by its sheer size; it stood 8 ft. tall. But most of all, I remember the raw power. It was equipped with a 7½-hp direct-drive motor, and the saw seemed unstoppable.

That bandsaw was produced for industrial use at a time when woodworking machines always seemed to have more than enough power. Today the trend seems to be to manufacture woodwork-

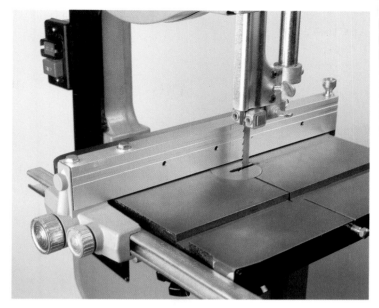

This fence easily adjusts and locks in place for secure ripping. The two bolts near the front allow you to set the fence so that it cuts a true parallel line. (Photo by Scott Phillips.)

ing machines with motors that meet minimum horsepower requirements. Many bandsaws have enough power for everyday applications, but when you raise the upper guide to the maximum height, you almost have to coax the blade through the cut.

Bandsaw motors range from the diminutive ⅕-hp motors found on some benchtop saws to the 10-hp motors on large industrial machines. Some consumer bandsaws in the 14-in. category come equipped with a 1-hp motor that often strains to get the job done, especially if you add a riser block. I know of one woodworker with a 14-in. bandsaw equipped with a riser block who is on his third motor. He began with the standard ½-hp motor and worked his way through successively larger motors. The 1-hp motor he has now seems up to the job: It's lasted eight years.

Bandsaw motors are mounted in one of three ways: directly to the shaft of the lower wheel, below the saw in a steel cabinet or stand, or mounted to the back of the bandsaw frame.

Direct-drive motors

The most basic method of turning the wheels on a bandsaw is with a direct-drive motor. Connecting the motor directly to the drive wheel is the most efficient method of turning the wheels. This method is used both on the smallest benchtop saws and on the largest industrial saws. There is no loss of power through heat and vibration, and this drive system doesn't suffer from belt slippage, out-of-round pulleys, or other similar problems that can sometimes plague belt-drive bandsaws. The fact that industrial bandsaws use direct-drive motors is one reason why they have such tremendous power and torque.

However, direct-drive bandsaws do have one potential drawback. If the motor ever fails, you're usually stuck buying a new motor from the saw's manufacturer. This is because direct-drive motors have mounts and drive connections that are unique to the machine for which they were designed. A stock motor from a supplier simply won't fit.

Motors mounted below the saw

The most common method of bandsaw motor mounting is underneath the saw in the cabinet or base that supports the saw. The motor mounts on a sheet-metal bracket that adjusts to tension the belt.

The belt transfers power to the lower wheel of the bandsaw by pulleys. When the pulleys are true and balanced, this design works just fine. Unfortunately, many saws come supplied with inexpensive die-cast pulleys that are not true or round, and the flimsy sheet-metal motor-mounting bracket flexes with each revolution of the out-of-round pulleys. The resulting vibrations make the saw difficult to use. Bandsaws with die-cast pulleys can be significantly improved by simply upgrading to machined pulleys.

Motors mounted to the frame

The third method of mounting the motor is to the back of the saw frame. A drive belt and pulleys are also used with this design, but the system is much more rigid and free of vibration. The face of the motor used in this system is fastened to the saw frame, and the motor shaft protrudes through a hole in the frame. The motor pulley is connected to the wheel pulley by a belt.

There are several advantages to this mounting system, which is far superior to mounting the motor in the base of the saw and makes the saw run smoothly. First, the transmission belt is much shorter, which reduces the energy lost through the vibration of a long belt. Second, face-mount motors have much more rigid mounting than motors set on a sheet-metal bracket. Finally, bandsaws that use this mounting system typically have cast-iron pulleys that have been machined true and round.

3 Buying a Bandsaw

There are many things to consider before buying a bandsaw, such as frame size and type, horsepower, and overall quality. A bandsaw is a major purchase that can cost hundreds or even thousands of dollars. In this chapter, I'll discuss the available options so that you can buy the best bandsaw for your woodworking style and budget.

What Size Saw?

When considering bandsaws, bigger is better. Large bandsaws can make the small, intricate cuts, but small saws can't make the big cuts. Large saws have greater height and throat capacity, which enable you to cut to the center of a large panel or to resaw a wide board.

Bandsaws fall into three types, depending on size. Benchtop models generally have wheel diameters smaller than 10 in., stand models range from 10 in. to 16 in., and floor-model bandsaws are from 16 in. up. Each size and type has its advantages and disadvantages.

But there is more to consider than just wheel diameter. You also need to think about the motor size and the blade size and its tension.

Benchtop bandsaws

Benchtop bandsaws are small, lightweight machines that may work well for fine cuts in relatively thin stock, but they simply lack the power and capacity for serious woodworking. Benchtop bandsaws are designed for small, delicate cuts. Their frames aren't stiff enough to properly tension a wide blade.

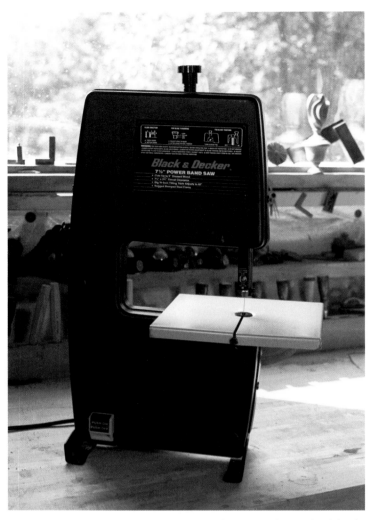

Benchtop saws are lightweight, with ribbed frames made from aluminum or plastic.

Benchtop blades

Don't use a wide blade on a benchtop bandsaw. The saw is designed for small, delicate cuts, and its frame isn't stiff enough to properly tension a wide blade.

Most benchtop saws have two wheels, but some have three. On two-wheel saws, the throat capacity is typically ¼ in. less than the wheel diameter (see the drawing on the facing page), but the throat of three-wheel bandsaws is much wider. Three-wheel saws have much greater throat capacity than two-wheel ones because the wheels form a triangle (see the drawing on p. 40). This design advantage allows a small three-wheel bandsaw to cut a fairly wide board, but this is its only advantage.

The biggest problem with three-wheel saws is that the frame isn't rigid enough to properly tension blades that are more than ⅜ in. wide. This is because the triangular frame design is inherently weak and can't apply the pressure that is needed to tension all but the smallest of blades. Without adequate tension, the blade flexes in a heavy cut and spoils the workpiece.

Another problem with three-wheel saws is that they tend to break blades. This is because the blade is severely stressed as it's flexed around the saw's small-diameter wheels. Manufacturers sidestep this problem by using a thinner 0.018-in. blade on their three-wheel saws. Of course, the thin blade is much more flexible than a standard 0.025-in. blade, which enables it to flex around the small wheels without breaking. However, blades less than 0.025 in. thick tend to flex and twist when cutting contours. This can make it difficult to saw to a line.

What Size Means

When talking about the size of a bandsaw, it's usual to refer to the wheel diameter. As shown in the drawing, the throat width limits the width of the stock you can run through your saw. The throat width is nearly the same as the wheel diameter but typically a little less since most saws use the frame to shield the blade. In most cases, the length and width of the table are similar to the wheel diameter.

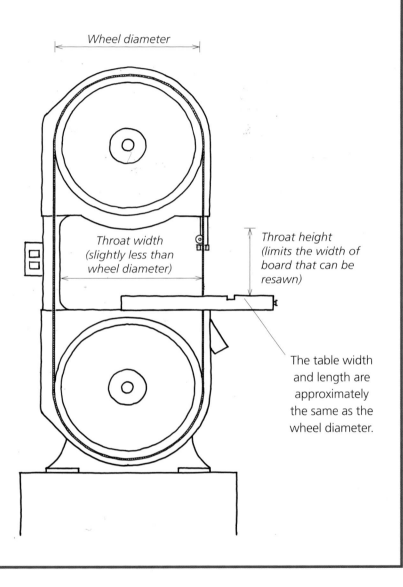

Wheel diameter

Throat width (slightly less than wheel diameter)

Throat height (limits the width of board that can be resawn)

The table width and length are approximately the same as the wheel diameter.

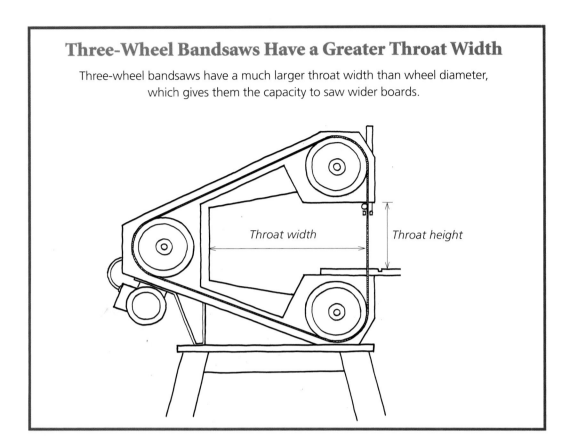

Three-Wheel Bandsaws Have a Greater Throat Width

Three-wheel bandsaws have a much larger throat width than wheel diameter, which gives them the capacity to saw wider boards.

Throat width

Throat height

Stand models

Bandsaws with a wheel diameter of 12 in. to 16 in. are mounted on a steel stand or an enclosed cabinet to raise the table to a comfortable working height (see the photo at left on the facing page). Delta introduced the first 14-in. consumer bandsaw in the 1940s. Since then, the design has become an icon of the home workshop and many small professional shops, too. It seems that almost every manufacturer makes a copy of Delta's famous saw. Of course, Delta is still producing the original of this well-known machine.

This style of saw has become extremely popular because of its low price and versatility. For the average woodworker who is cutting curves and occasionally resawing, 14-in. bandsaws are a great value. As an added benefit, most of them can accept a riser block that doubles the resaw capacity to 12 in. (see the photo at right on the facing page). If you are shopping for a bandsaw in this category, realize that although many of these saws look the same, they are not all created equal. It's worth your time and effort to compare bandsaws before you buy. I suggest that you narrow the field down to those saws that can accept a ¾-in.-wide blade and have a motor of at least 1 hp.

The 14-in. stand-model bandsaw has become an icon of the home and small professional shop. Its cost is reasonable, yet the bandsaw is large enough to handle serious resawing.

The cutting height on this bandsaw has been increased by adding a riser block, which can be seen just to the right of the table.

If you are just starting out and have never owned a bandsaw, the saws in this category are a great choice. They're inexpensive and compact yet large enough for most tasks in the average shop.

Floor models

Floor-model bandsaws range in size from 18 in. to 42 in. Their large frames, tables, and motors make these saws the true workhorses among bandsaws. Floor-model bandsaws are designed for resawing and continuous cutting of heavy stock, but they will also make delicate cuts. That's what makes floor-model bandsaws so versatile. Most bandsaws in this category accept blades as narrow as ⅛ in. and as wide as 1 in., and the largest floor-model saws can accept blades as wide as 2 in. To tension such wide blades, floor-model saws are designed with heavy frames, cast-iron wheels, massive wheel bearings, and stout tension screws with Acme-style threads.

What's Big Enough?

You're probably asking, "How big a bandsaw do I really need?" Ultimately, the answer depends on the type of woodworking that you do.

If you plan to do a lot of resawing, I recommend buying at least an 18-in. floor-model bandsaw. Most floor-model bandsaws should be able to crank out enough tension, but to be sure, ask the manufacturers if they've taken measurements with a tension meter. A couple of manufacturers I spoke to admitted they had never tested their bandsaws with a tension meter to see how much tension the frame could actually apply to a blade.

The 14-in. bandsaws are very popular because of their reasonable price and moderate cutting capacity. As an added advantage, most 14-in. saws will accept a riser block that doubles their cutting height. I owned a 14-in. bandsaw for many years, so I speak from experience when I say that they're a great choice for most woodworkers.

If you choose to buy one of the 14-in. consumer bandsaws, I suggest buying the largest motor available for it. You'll get good resaw performance out of the saw if you don't use blades wider than ½ in.

In the 1970s, when I bought my 14-in. bandsaw, my choices were limited to either a huge, expensive industrial machine or a 14-in. saw. Today, however, steel-frame bandsaws from Italy are hot contenders.

Italian bandsaws are larger and more powerful than any 14-in. saw, and they are very smooth running. Best of all, they're affordable. For not much more than you would have to pay for a better-quality 14-in. bandsaw equipped with a riser block, motor upgrade, and fence, you can get a 16-in. steel-frame bandsaw. The 16-in. saw has more power, capacity, and frame stiffness for tensioning wide resaw blades.

If you can afford an 18-in. saw, so much the better. Large bandsaws are much more versatile than small ones. But large bandsaws have disadvantages, too; the most obvious one being price. Fortunately, as the popularity of woodworking has increased, machinery prices have become more competitive. Used bandsaws are an option worth exploring, too.

For years the frames of floor-model bandsaws were made of cast iron—and many still are. Cast iron is heavy and strong, features that make it well suited for tensioning wide blades and absorbing vibration. But casting frames from iron is costly, and the expense has always placed large bandsaws out of the price range of many woodworkers.

Large floor-model bandsaws can handle delicate cuts well as a small saw, but they also have the power and capacity to resaw a wide hardwood board. Bigger saw are more versatile than small saws.

In recent years, several companies have begun manufacturing steel-frame bandsaws, and many are imported from Europe. The frames on these bandsaws are fabricated from heavy-gauge sheet steel that is folded and welded. Although not inexpensive, steel-frame bandsaws are within a price range that is affordable to many woodworkers.

Resaw bandsaws are a type of floor-model bandsaw specifically designed with 2½-in.- to 3-in.-wide blades for continuous heavy-duty resawing of boards as well as veneer (see the photo at right below). Although some of these bandsaws can accept narrow blades for contour cutting, this normally requires the purchase of an additional set of guides. These saws were

A large floor-model bandsaw with a welded-steel frame generally costs less than a comparable saw with a cast-iron frame. With good design and engineering, a steel-frame bandsaw can be every bit as good as a cast-iron model.

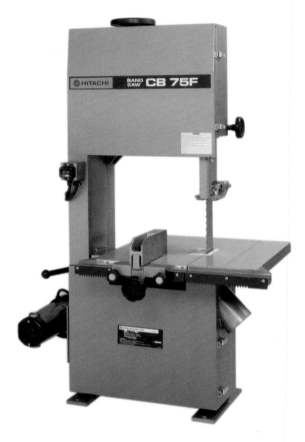

A resaw bandsaw is stiff enough to handle the tension a 2-in. resaw blade requires for top performance. Although this bandsaw is out of the price range of most small shops, it's a worthwhile addition to any shop that makes a lot of veneer or does considerable resawing. (Photo courtesy Hitachi Power Tools USA, Ltd.)

meant to be used as dedicated resaw machines by shops that do a lot of resawing and veneer making. You'll probably want to make certain you'll be feeding a resaw machine a steady diet of wide boards before you open your checkbook.

Motor sizes

The motor on a bandsaw plays a critical role in the saw's ability to cut through dense, thick stock. Bandsaw motor sizes range from ⅕ hp on little benchtop saws to 10 hp on 36-in. industrial saws. So how much power do you really need? It depends on the type of woodworking you do. Cutting curves in furniture parts obviously requires very little power, but continuous resawing of wide stock consumes quite a lot.

Many of the popular 14-in. bandsaws come equipped with a ¾-hp motor that

works well for most situations on this size of machine. But if you increase the saw's height capacity to 12 in. with a riser block, you may find a ¾-hp motor to be anemic. I'm not saying that the motor won't power the blade through 12 in. of dense hardwood, but you'll just have to be patient and feed the stock very slowly. Coaxing the saw may be okay for an occasional cut, but if you plan to saw a lot of thick stock, I suggest buying a saw with a 1-hp motor—or better yet a larger bandsaw with 2 hp to 3 hp.

Blade sizes and tensions

If you intend to resaw many wide boards, you need to understand the demands accurate resawing puts on a bandsaw. Resawing is best done with a wide blade; the wider the better. Although it is possible to perform limited resawing with a ⅜-in. or even a ¼-in. blade, resawing is much faster and more precise with a ¾-in. or 1-in. blade.

A wide blade is desirable because its greater beam strength resists bending under load (see the drawing on the facing page). Although beam strength may seem an odd term to use in this case, it comes from the fact that a bandsaw blade supported by two guides with the feed pressure somewhere in the middle of the span is, in engineering terms, a beam. Think of a floor joist, which is also another relatively narrow beam. A joist is suspended from its ends, and it's oriented on edge with the widest part of the board perpen-

Because it's 150% wider than the ½-in.-wide blade at right, the 1¼-in. resaw blade at left has greater beam strength. That means it requires more force to achieve proper tension.

dicular to the floor. If joists were hung with the wide part parallel to the floor, they'd sag. The stiffness comes from the width being perpendicular to the load. The same idea applies to bandsaw blades. Greater beam strength comes from width, not thickness.

But beam strength also comes from having sufficient tension on the blade. Therefore, it is not enough for a bandsaw to be capable of accepting a wide blade; it must also be able to tension it properly. This is where many consumer bandsaws fail.

Here are the facts: An ordinary carbon-steel blade requires 15,000 psi (pounds per square inch) of tension for maximum beam strength. Bimetal, carbide-tipped, and spring-steel blades need much more for proper tension—25,000 psi. In my experience, I've found that many consumer bandsaws just can't crank out that much tension, particularly on a 3/4-in.-wide blade. To satisfy my curiosity, I tested several well-known brands of 14-in. bandsaws.

To achieve 15,000 psi on a 1/2-in.-wide carbon-steel blade, all the saws had to be tensioned well beyond the mark for 3/4-in. blades on the saw-tension gauge. In fact, I had to totally compress the tension spring to get the proper tension.

None of the consumer bandsaws I tested were capable of properly tensioning a 3/4-in.-wide blade despite the calibration marks on the tension scale. The frames on the saws were simply not stiff

enough to apply 25,000 psi to even a 1/2-in.-wide blade—much less a 3/4-in.-wide blade.

I've also subjected several large steel-frame bandsaws to the same test. The only difference was that I used a 1-in.-wide bimetal blade, which takes considerably more force than a 1/2-in.-wide blade to properly tension. All the bandsaws I tested had wheel diameters of 18 in. or more. Each of the steel-frame bandsaws was easily able to tension the 1-in.-wide blade to 30,000 psi.

Of course, the ability to apply the correct amount of tension

Blade size

Most midsize bandsaws can't properly tension a 3/4-in. resaw blade. Rather than use a wide blade that you can't tension properly, use a high-performance 1/2-in. or even 3/8-in. blade.

Wider Blades Have Greater Beam Strength

The greater fore-and-aft dimension of a wide bandsaw blade makes it stiffer and less likely to bend when stock is fed into the blade.

Narrow blade   **Wide blade**

Feed pressure

How Much Tension Is Really Necessary?

You may be wondering if bandsaw blades really need that much tension. Blade manufacturers recommend 15,000 psi for a carbon-steel blade and 25,000 psi for a bimetal, spring-steel, or carbide-tipped blade. Following these guidelines will give the blades maximum beam strength when sawing stock of maximum thickness, such as when resawing or slicing veneer from a wide board. Beam strength is needed to keep the blade from flexing and spoiling your stock.

Of course, you can apply much less tension to the blade for less demanding sawing, such as when cutting contours in 1-in.- to 2-in.-thick stock. Cutting stock less than 2 in. thick doesn't place nearly as much load on the blade as when cutting thicker stock.

Changing blades

If you take full advantage of your bandsaw's versatility, you'll change blades frequently. Look for features that make the process as quick and easy as possible.

doesn't necessarily mean that a bandsaw will run properly. If the wheels or frame are distorted during the tensioning process, a blade may not track on the tires, so I checked each of the bandsaws by making cuts on thick stock. All of the saws tracked perfectly.

Blade-Changing Considerations

Most woodworkers probably don't consider the ease of changing blades when shopping for a bandsaw, but the process isn't as quick and easy as changing table-saw blades. It's more like changing a tire on your car. Consider this: When you change a bandsaw blade, you must disconnect the saw from its electrical source, open the covers, release the blade tension, remove the blade, install a new blade, tension the blade, track the blade, adjust the upper and lower guides, adjust the upper and lower thrust wheels, and close the covers. If you've ever changed a bandsaw blade, you already know what I'm talking about. To make this time-consuming chore faster, here are a few features to look for when buying a new bandsaw.

Hinged covers
Hinged covers help make blade changing a snap (see the top right photo on the facing page). These covers quickly swing out of the way, as opposed to covers that must be removed from the saw. My old Delta bandsaw had removable covers, and each cover was secured with two threaded knobs that also had to be removed before the covers would come off. Needless to say, I avoided changing blades.

Quick-release catches
This small feature also decreases the time needed to change blades (see the photo at left on the facing page). Although most bandsaws today have some type of quick-

This 14-in. bandsaw has hinged wheel covers that make removing and replacing blades a snap.

This quick-release catch just pivots to open the wheel cover. It's a small point, but every detail makes it easier to use your bandsaw to its fullest capacity.

release catch on the cover, some still use a threaded knob or screw that takes more time to remove.

Large, easy-to-reach tension handwheels

A large, accessible tension handwheel is another great feature that effectively cuts down on the time needed to change blades (see the bottom photo at right). Manufacturers, are you listening?

Easy table-slot alignment

Bandsaw tables must have a slot in the casting to allow for blade changing. To help keep the two halves aligned, some type of fastener is used at the table edge.

A large tension handwheel that's easy to grip makes cranking in blade tension faster and easier.

Some saws use a tapered pin that can be quickly removed without tools. To prevent you from misplacing the pin, some manufacturers attach it to the bandsaw with a wire cable. Other saws have a screw for table alignment, but a screw is slower to remove than a tapered pin. But without a doubt, the worst mechanism for table alignment is a rail. The rail is typically attached with four screws to the table edge. Unfortunately, I once owned a saw that used this method, so I speak from experience.

Removing this slotted blade guard is quick and easy. All you have to do is back off the hex-head machine screws.

Hinged or slotted blade guards

A guard is attached to the guidepost to shield the blade. The guard is for your safety and should not be removed permanently. However, it typically must be removed temporarily when switching to a wide blade. The best guards are hinged and quickly swing out of the way. Others must be removed from the saw entirely; if this is the case, it's best if the mounting holes in the guard are slotted (see the top photo at left). This way you can simply loosen the two screws that secure the guard and slip it off the guidepost.

Foot brakes

The heavy cast-iron wheels on large bandsaws develop so much inertia that they can take a couple of minutes to coast to a stop. A foot brake will stop the saw quickly so that you can change blades or make guide adjustments (see the bottom photo at left).

Choosing Guides

There are two types of bandsaw guides: blocks and bearings. Woodworkers who prefer bearings often tout blocks as inferior, but this isn't necessarily true. Block guides do an excellent job of supporting the blade. In some ways blocks provide better support than bearings. The only disadvantage to blocks is that they wear and occasionally need to be squared up with a file.

All guide blocks used to be steel, but today there are several softer composite materials that are sometimes used in place

A foot brake will stop the wheels quickly to allow blade changes and adjustments.

of steel. I believe steel is still the best choice for guide blocks because the newer materials quickly wear out and need frequent replacing. You may have heard that steel guide blocks heat up the blade and shorten its life, but this isn't really true. The small amount of heat generated from guide-block friction may cause the blade to expand somewhat. If this occurs, the blade will need retensioning. However, excessive heat is generated at the tooth tip as a result of cutting thick, dense wood or feeding the stock too slowly. This occurs regardless of the type of guide used.

There are two types of bearing guides, American-style and European-style (see pp. 30-31). Both work equally well, although I've found that the European guides are faster and easier to adjust. This is because European guides have large, knurled adjustment screws and locking rings so they don't require tools.

Although they are a nice feature, bearing guides can add unnecessary expense to the price of a new saw. They will obviously run cooler than steel block guides will, but this is only a factor in industrial settings where bandsaws run continuously under heavy loads. The downside to bearings is that they don't support the blade as close to the stock as it's being cut as guide blocks do. The point at which bearings support the blade is at a distance equal to one-half the bearing diameter (see the drawing on p. 50). However, guide blocks support the blade directly above the stock (see the photo on p. 50). Although this difference may seem minor, it becomes most apparent when

European bearing guides offer excellent support for the blade, and they are the guides that are the easiest to adjust.

The bearings on American-made Carter bearing guides are oriented differently than those on European guides. The blade is tangent to the rotation.

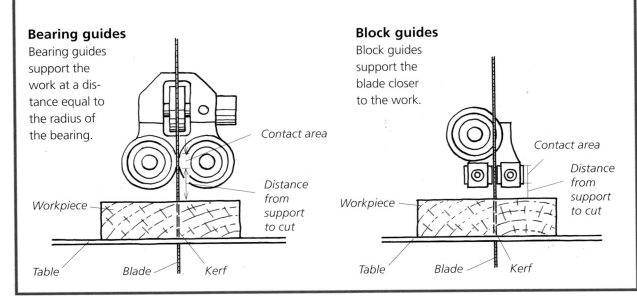

Guide Blocks Provide the Most Support

Because it is round, a bearing makes contact with the blade only in a small area tangent to the bearing, whereas blocks have a much larger surface area in contact with the blade. In addition, the shapes of the blocks and their mounting brackets make it possible to lower the guides closer to the workpiece, which means the blade is supported closer to the actual cut.

Bearing guides
Bearing guides support the work at a distance equal to the radius of the bearing.

Contact area

Distance from support to cut

Workpiece

Table   Blade   Kerf

Block guides
Block guides support the blade closer to the work.

Contact area

Distance from support to cut

Workpiece

Table   Blade   Kerf

Guide blocks have the advantage of supporting the blade closer to the stock than is possible with bearing guides.

you're cutting contours because the blade flexes more through twists and turns when supported by bearing guides.

Rating Overall Quality

It seems that almost every woodworking-machine manufacturer makes at least one bandsaw. As you flip through the pages of your favorite woodworking magazine, you're sure to see plenty of ads. This is good news for woodworkers. Over the years, I've noticed that the competition has caused the quality and selection of bandsaws to dramatically improve from

This wheel has been balanced for smooth performance. The indication is the drill mark where a small amount of material was removed.

what it was 20 years ago. However, there are still a few bandsaws out there to avoid.

There are a number of ways to judge the quality of a bandsaw, but I think that one of the best indications is the smoothness of the saw as it is running. Bandsaws have more rotating parts than most woodworking machines—tires, wheels, and pulleys—and they all must be trued and balanced if the saw is going to run smoothly. If you've ever used a vibrating bandsaw, then you know how difficult and annoying working with it can be. In fact, I've used bandsaws that vibrate so badly that it was difficult to follow the layout line when cutting.

Wheels may be cast from iron or aluminum, and the rim must be turned true and concentric to the shaft hole. After truing the wheel, it should be balanced (see the top photo at right). The most accurate results are achieved from dynamic balancing because the wheel is checked for balance as it rotates. This is similar to the way your car's tires are balanced. Static balancing can also work well if done carefully. Unfortunately, some manufacturers of consumer bandsaws don't even bother with balancing the wheels.

Another key to bandsaw smoothness is the quality of the drive pulleys. Pulleys are either cast iron or die-cast. The best pulleys are cast as well as turned true and concentric with the shaft hole (see the bottom photo at right).

There are other quality checkpoints as well. One of the most critical is the guide-

Preventing vibration

When turning parts, such as pulleys and wheels, aren't round and true, a saw will have so much vibration that the smoothness and accuracy of the cut will suffer. A quick way to scope out overall quality is to check the wheels and pulleys to see if they've been machined and balanced.

A close inspection reveals concentric rings on the surface of this pulley. This extra step in machining makes the pulley run smoothly.

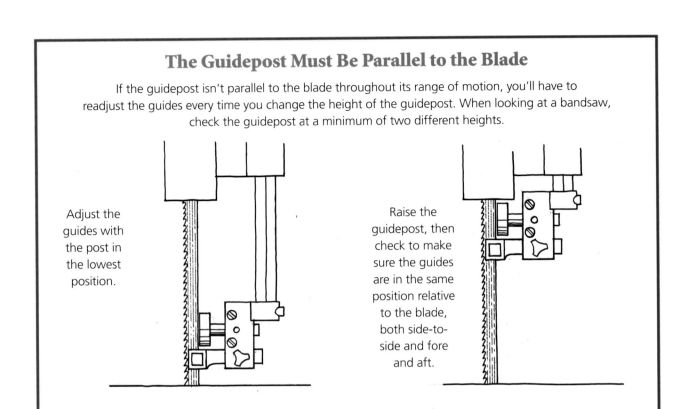

The Guidepost Must Be Parallel to the Blade

If the guidepost isn't parallel to the blade throughout its range of motion, you'll have to readjust the guides every time you change the height of the guidepost. When looking at a bandsaw, check the guidepost at a minimum of two different heights.

Adjust the guides with the post in the lowest position.

Raise the guidepost, then check to make sure the guides are in the same position relative to the blade, both side-to-side and fore and aft.

A good table

A flat table is essential for true ripping and quality joinery. Check the table of any saw you're considering buying by placing a straightedge in several places on the table and by looking for light beneath it.

post. The guidepost should be sturdy and rigid, but most important, it should be parallel to the blade throughout its travel. For best results, it's important to check the guidepost in at least two positions (see the drawing above). To get an accurate reading, the post should be locked each time it

is repositioned. If the guidepost isn't parallel to the blade, you'll have to painstakingly readjust the upper guides every time you make a height adjustment.

Another sign of quality is a flat, sturdy table. The table casting should be thick and heavily ribbed so that it won't flex under the load of a heavy workpiece. If you examine the underside of the table, the ribs should appear as a crisscross pattern of extra iron in the casting. As you tilt the table, it should travel smoothly and lock firmly in position. Make sure there is enough room for your hands to operate the table-tilt lock knobs.

If the bandsaw is mounted on a stand, it should be stiff, rigid, and fully capable of supporting the saw without twisting or flexing.

Shopping for a New Bandsaw

Bandsaws tend to look the same when pictured in advertisements. Sometimes different brand names appear as though they came from the same factory. I suspect that some of them do. But there is definitely a substantial difference in similar-looking bandsaws when it comes to performance.

I suggest you begin by requesting literature from several manufacturers of bandsaws that you're interested in. You can use the toll-free numbers provided in the Sources section (see p. 196) to request information from manufacturers.

After narrowing the field, I would view the bandsaws firsthand. Many large cities have specialty woodworking stores with large machinery displays from several manufacturers, or you could attend one of the many woodworking shows that crisscross the country. Still another option is to visit the shops of woodworking friends, view their bandsaws, and ask their opinions.

A sturdy stand

If you're considering a midsize bandsaw on a sheet-metal stand, run the saw to make sure the stand is sturdy enough to resist flexing under load. If the stand isn't rigid enough, you can build a sturdy plywood base and fill it with sand.

Checklist for Buying a New Bandsaw

With the market for bandsaws so competitive, the only way you can sort out the good saws from the bad is to shop carefully. Here's a checklist for you to use when comparing new bandsaws.

Bandsaw make and model: _____

Date inspected: _____

Dealer: _____

Phone: _____

Price and options included: _____

_____

☐ **Frame strength:** Will this frame properly tension the widest blade that the bandsaw accepts? Ask the manufacturer if it has tested the saw at the recommended tension.

☐ **Throat capacity:** Will this bandsaw handle the widest stock I intend to cut?

☐ **Height capacity:** Does this bandsaw have the resaw capacity that I need?

☐ **Minimum blade width:** Can this bandsaw handle the 1/16-in. or 1/8-in. blades needed for cutting tight contours?

☐ **Maximum blade width:** Will this saw accept a blade wide enough for resawing (1/2 in. or more)?

☐ **Motor horsepower:** Does this saw have a minimum of 1 hp for resawing?

☐ **Blade guide type:** Does this bandsaw have the guides I prefer?

☐ **Table tilt:** Does the table tilt in one direction or two? How far will it tilt?

☐ **Comments:**

I have always been careful to examine and compare tools before I buy. Besides researching the machine, I also like to know a few things about the service provided after the sale. Here are the questions I typically ask.

- How long is the warranty?
- Does the warranty cover labor as well as parts?

- If the bandsaw is found to be defective immediately upon unpacking (this happens more frequently than you may think), is there help available or am I responsible for transporting the machine many miles to a service center?
- How close is the nearest service center?
- For how many years will parts be available for the bandsaw?

Although it looks a little rough, this 20-in. bandsaw needed only a good cleaning and a new set of tires. The price was less than half that of a new 14-in. saw.

Shopping for a Used Bandsaw

Shopping for a used bandsaw can be a great way to get the saw you're looking for at a bargain price. Good used woodworking equipment in running condition can often be found at a fraction of the price of a new machine. Through the years I've bought several used machines, and each time I was able to get a great tool and save a lot of money.

But shopping for a used bandsaw is also a way to get stuck with expensive junk. Many bandsaws offered for sale are simply worn out. Others may be missing costly parts or the much-needed part may no longer be available. Any machine made before 1950 is generally not worth pursuing. You may have heard people lament that they don't make them like they used to. It's a good thing they don't! As a rule, newer bandsaws have more efficient designs, better bearings, better balancing of rotating parts, and they are safer, too. Newer bandsaws may not be as heavy as the old machines, but they don't necessarily need to be.

I remember looking at a large, used bandsaw years ago. I owned a 12-in. bandsaw at the time and the newspaper ad stated that this was a 20-in. saw. The price was right, too. I excitedly followed the directions I was given over the phone, and in just a few minutes I was looking at a dusty, old 20-in. cast-iron bandsaw. It had a few problems like worn tires and a missing guide, but for the price the saw was a bargain in need of a few hours of work. I had found just what I had hoped for—until I spotted the crack. Actually, I felt it as I was running my hand up the saw's column toward the upper wheel. The crack in the saw's iron casting was large enough that I feared the saw's wheels would never align properly. Of course, a skilled welder could have repaired the crack, but that was no guarantee that a blade would ever track properly again, so I decided to pass. It's possible to find a bargain on a used bandsaw, but you must know what to look for as well as what to avoid.

A good place to begin looking for a used bandsaw is in the classified section of many woodworking magazines. There you'll find tools for sale from individuals as well as dealers who specialize in used machines. Dealers often have a large selection of bandsaws on hand. If they don't have a bandsaw to meet your needs, they're usually willing to take your name and call you when they get one.

Auctions are another source for used bandsaws. When large furniture plants go out of business, often the entire inventory

Checklist for Buying a Used Bandsaw

When you're looking at a used bandsaw, go slowly and try to be objective. This checklist will help.

Bandsaw make and model: _____
Date inspected: _____
Seller: _____
Phone: _____

☐ Is the saw missing any parts? If so, list them and research the replacement cost: _____

☐ Does the motor run? If not, list the model number and research the replacement cost: _____
_____

☐ Is the motor a single-phase or a three-phase one? Do you need a phase converter?

☐ Inspect the bearings (motor and wheel). Does the bandsaw have babbitt bearings? List those needing replacement and research the cost: _____
_____

☐ Inspect the frame by hand for cracks and welds.

☐ Do the tires need replacement? List details and research the cost of new tires as well as the cost of sending the wheels out to have new tires fitted: _____
_____

☐ Check the upper and lower guide adjustments. Do the guides need to be replaced? If so, list details and research the replacement cost: _____
_____

☐ Is the guidepost parallel to the blade?

☐ How does the saw run under power and under load?

☐ Comments:

This direct-drive, three-phase motor will need a phase converter to run on single-phase current. By the time you purchase the phase converter and possibly upgrade your electrical system to handle it, this saw may no longer be a bargain.

Buying used

If you buy a used bandsaw from a dealer, the machine is almost always in good working order. You get support after the sale, and many dealers even offer a short warranty.

of machines is offered for sale. Be careful, however—it's easy to get caught up in the bidding frenzy and pay more than you planned. Also, machines sold at auction are "as is," so get there early to have ample time to thoroughly examine any bandsaws you may be interested in.

Check any saw you're serious about for missing parts. Minor items can be easily replaced, as can broken or missing guides, but if the saw is missing a major component (such as the table or a wheel), you may be out of luck. If the saw is less than 30 years old and made by a major manufacturer, parts may still be available, but check the prices first—you may be in for a surprise.

It may not seem like a big deal if the saw needs a new motor, but it can be. If the saw is belt driven, you can typically swap out a three-phase motor of 5 hp or less for a single-phase motor. Most old industrial machines have direct-drive three-phase motors (see the photo at left). You can't just swap a three-phase motor for an equivalent single-phase motor. You'll have to buy an expensive phase converter to turn single-phase power into three-phase power before it gets to the motor. It's a good idea to have the seller run the machine before you make a purchase. A bandsaw that needs expensive repairs on an old three-phase direct-drive motor may not be a bargain.

When inspecting a machine, you should also spin the motor shaft by hand and check for bearing roughness, noise, and excessive play. Inspect the wheel bearings the same way. All bearings need eventual replacement, so if the bandsaw is very old, you may want to check the price (and availability) of new bearings. I would avoid any bandsaw with babbitt bearings. Babbitt metal is a soft alloy that is heated until molten, then poured around the shaft of the machine to form a bearing in place. It's a very old style of bearing and a real pain. I've used many old machines with babbitt bearings. They require continual oiling, and the oil is often slung out of the bearing and onto your clothes, your work, and anything else that may be within striking distance.

Next, inspect the frame by hand. Avoid any saw with cracks or welds in the frame, even small ones, since most small cracks eventually become big. Just because a crack has been welded is no guarantee that you won't have problems in the future. Once a frame has been cracked, it may be nearly impossible to get the saw's wheels in proper alignment again.

Tires must be smooth and free of cracks or missing chunks. New tires are available to fit almost any bandsaw, but they are not easy to install. Also, once you've got the tires on the wheels, you may have to crown them. This can be a tedious job, so you may want to send the wheels out for this work. Check the cost.

Check to see that all the adjustments on the guides are smooth and that there are no missing parts. Aftermarket block or bearing guides can be ordered for most any bandsaw, new or old. Guides, like cars, have gotten much more compact

Although this old guide is in good working order, a new replacement guide is more compact and will increase cutting height.

over the years. You may gain a couple of extra inches of height capacity by replacing a bulky, old upper guide (see Sources on pp. 196-197).

Regardless of where you shop for a used bandsaw, it's important to examine the machine carefully and see it under power and load.

Bandsaw Blades

It didn't take long after buying my first bandsaw for me to realize the importance of having the right bandsaw blade. It is, without a doubt, the most important part of any bandsaw. This is true regardless of whether you own an inexpensive home-shop bandsaw or the finest industrial-grade bandsaw. An average bandsaw will cut much better with a great blade, but the finest bandsaw will disappoint you if it has the wrong blade.

Because there's such a number of blade styles to choose from, selecting the right blade can at first seem confusing. But the versatility that we all desire from our bandsaws depends entirely on selecting the proper blade for the job at hand. Most of us (myself included) probably mount a 50-tooth alternate-top bevel (ATB) combo blade on our table saws and leave it there until it needs resharpening. That

one blade will effectively miter, rip, cross-cut, and do just about anything else we need it to do. It doesn't work that way on the bandsaw, where the blades are much more specialized. The best blade for cutting the contours of a cabriole leg won't accurately resaw veneer.

In this chapter, I'll discuss what you need to know about putting together an arsenal of blades for your own bandsaw that's appropriate for the woodwork you intend to do. All blades share a common terminology, so start with the sidebar on p. 60 to learn the language. Many factors are involved in selecting the right blade for the job, so I'll give you some specific examples. I'll also talk about cleaning your blades to improve their performance, how to safely coil and uncoil a bandsaw blade, and finally, what's involved in welding your own blades.

The variety of blades available is the key to the bandsaw's versatility. From left to right: ⅛ in., 18 pitch; ¼ in., 10 pitch; ¼ in., 6 pitch; ⅜ in., 3/4 pitch, carbide-tipped; ¾ in., 3 pitch; ¾ in., 2 pitch.

Bands of Steel

Woodworking tools such as sawblades, router bits, and shaper cutterheads have greatly improved over the years, and bandsaw blades are no exception. The materials and manufacturing processes used to produce bandsaw blades are extremely sophisticated. The blades available today are stronger, cut smoother, and stay sharp longer than ever before. They also cut with greater efficiency and less feed resistance.

Bandsaw blades perform a very demanding job. The back must be soft and pliable to flex around the wheels of the bandsaw several hundred revolutions each minute, yet the teeth must be hard to resist dulling while cutting. The harder and thicker the stock, the more quickly the teeth lose their edge.

To make the teeth hard and resistant to wear, manufacturers use one of three methods. In the first method, the teeth are cut into the band, set, and then hardened. This is done on carbon-steel and spring-steel blades. In the second method, a band of high-speed steel is welded to a softer back band, and the teeth are cut into the harder steel. These are called bimetal blades.

The third method is for carbide blades. Individual carbide teeth are brazed to a flexible steel band. Carbide blades are the most expensive because of the high cost of the material and the process used in making them. As you might expect, each of the three blade types has advantages and disadvantages. I'll discuss them individually.

Expect to change blades often

To get the most out of your bandsaw, you'll have to change blades often from wide to narrow or from few teeth to many. Each type of blade is best for a certain kind of cutting.

Welds

Bandsaw-blade stock is manufactured in long lengths, then individual blades are cut to length and welded together. The weld is important to blade life and performance. For best results, a weld must be strong, flexible, and smooth. A smooth weld is flush on the sides and back and free of excess flash. This allows the weld to travel through the guides without catching and breaking.

Bandsaw-Blade Terms

Bladeback: The body of the blade not including the tooth. The back of the blade must be both tough and pliable to withstand the continuous flexing as the blade runs around the wheels of the saw.

Gullet: The curved area at the base of the tooth that carries away the sawdust. The size and efficiency of the gullets decrease as the pitch is increased.

Pitch: The number of teeth per inch (tpi) as measured from the tips of the teeth. The pitch determines the feed rate at which the blade can cut and the smoothness of the sawn surface. Pitch can be either constant or variable.

Rake angle: The angle of the face of the tooth measured in respect to a line drawn perpendicular to the cutting direction. Regular and skip blades have a zero rake angle, which gives them a slow, scraping action. Hook blades have a positive rake angle, which causes them to cut more aggressively.

Set: The bending of the sawteeth to the left and right to create a kerf that is wider than the back. This prevents the back from binding in the cut. Carbide teeth are not bent; they are simply wider than the steel band to which they are brazed.

Thickness: The thickness of the steel band measured at the blade back. In general, thick blades are wider and stiffer than thin blades. Thicker blades require larger-diameter bandsaw wheels to prevent stress cracks and premature blade breakage.

Tooth: The cutting portion of the blade. Teeth must be sharp, hard, and resistant to both heat and wear.

Tooth tip: The sharp part of the tooth that shears away the wood fibers. During sawing, the tooth tip is under tremendous stress and subject to both heat and wear. The heat produced from friction during sawing can sometimes rise to 400°F on the tip of the tooth. This occurs because the wood insulates the blade during cutting.

Width: The dimension of a blade from the back of the band to the tip of the tooth. Wider blades are stiffer and resist side-to-side flexing, making them the best choice for resawing. Narrow blades can cut tighter contours.

Parts of a Bandsaw Blade

Bladeback

Pitch (number of teeth in 1 in.)

1 in.

Rake angle (0° on this blade)

Weld

Gullet

Tooth tip

Tooth

Set

Thickness

Width

Carbon steel

The most common bandsaw blades are made entirely of carbon steel. Carbon-steel blades are very popular and can be found in many forms in almost every consumer woodworking catalog. They're also the least expensive type of blade, especially when you purchase 100-ft. spools and weld or braze blades to fit your bandsaw.

Carbon-steel blades are sharp, cut well when new, and are available in a variety of widths and tooth forms. They are also inexpensive, which is probably the major reason for their popularity. The main disadvantage to carbon-steel blades is that they dull rather quickly, particularly when used for demanding applications such as resawing.

Sawing thick hardwood stock places the greatest demands on any blade. If the tooth tip becomes too hot, it becomes soft and quickly loses both its edge and set. Once the set and sharpness are lost, the blade deflects during cutting. The result is that the expensive stock you're sawing is ruined. For these reasons, I use narrow carbon-steel bandsaw blades only for less-demanding bandsaw applications such as sawing contours.

Spring steel

Spring steel is most often associated with the cheap, stamped-out blades found on new benchtop bandsaws. Spring steel is soft and flexible, which allows it to flex around the small-diameter wheels of benchtop saws. But because spring steel is so soft, it doesn't hold an edge for very long.

Sharpness

There are certainly varying degrees of sharpness among bandsaw blades. Sharpness depends on the quality of the grinding process used, which should leave each tooth smooth and free of burrs. The type of tooth material is also a factor. The high-speed steel in a bimetal blade can be ground sharper than carbide.

More important than initial sharpness is the extent to which a blade will retain its sharpness. Because carbide is so hard, it's extremely resistant to wear. However, carbon steel is not. Carbon steel works well for general-purpose work, such as cutting contours and stock less than 2 in. thick, but it loses its edge quickly when resawing. The heat at the tooth tip soon softens it, and the edge wears away.

Several years ago, however, a unique spring-steel resaw blade was introduced into the consumer market. Instead of being stamped, the teeth on this blade are carefully ground, hardened, and polished. The teeth have a variable spacing that limits harmonic vibration. These blades cut smooth, and best of all, the kerf is a mere $1/32$ in., which is approximately half the kerf of a typical carbide or carbon-steel blade. This means you'll get more veneer and less waste out of each plank. Additionally, because the blade is 0.022-in.-thick spring steel it will easily flex around the medium-size wheels of consumer bandsaws. This blade is marketed under the trade name The Wood Slicer (see Sources on pp. 196-197).

Bimetal

Bimetal blades are very different from carbon-steel blades and carbide-tipped blades in the way in which they are made.

Bandsaw-Blade Materials

Material	Cost	Advantages	Disadvantages	Best use
Stamped spring steel	Very inexpensive	• Very flexible for use on bandsaws with small-diameter wheels	• Stamped teeth dull very quickly	Light-duty cuts on small bandsaws
Carbon steel	Inexpensive	• Weld or braze your own • Readily available	• Dulls quickly • Cannot be sharpened	Cutting contours in relatively thin stock
Wood Slicer spring steel	Moderate	• Flexible, thin kerf • Ground teeth are polished and hardened • Variable pitch reduces vibration		Resawing
Bimetal	Moderate	• Cobalt-steel teeth don't overheat as readily as carbon-steel teeth • High recommended tension means greater beam strength		Demanding applications that generate a lot of heat such as resawing and cutting thick stock
Carbide	Moderately expensive	• Smooth cut because carbide teeth are precisely ground on all sides • Recommended tension is almost twice of that of carbon steel • Outlasts carbon-steel blades 25 to 1	• Cost • Carbide is brittle	Resawing and other demanding applications
Stellite	Very expensive	• Less brittle than carbide	• Cost • Not as hard as carbide	Resawing

Bimetal blades are actually two steel ribbons that are welded together (see the drawing at right). The back of a bimetal blade is composed of soft, flexible steel; the blade front, where the teeth are milled, is made of much harder high-speed steel.

This combination produces a relatively inexpensive blade with longer wear than ordinary carbon-steel blades. The teeth of carbon-steel blades lose their sharpness and set when overheated during resawing. However, the cobalt-steel teeth of a bimetal blade can withstand 1200°F, far more than the 400°F that damages the teeth of a carbon-steel blade.

Another advantage of a bimetal blade is the strength of its spring-steel back. The recommended tension is 25,000 psi. (Remember that greater tension increases the beam strength of a blade.) The beam strength of bimetal blades combined with their resistance to heat has endeared bimetal blades to many woodworkers.

Carbide

I'm sure that almost every woodworker is familiar with carbide. Carbide-tipped cutting tools have almost made high-speed steel tools things of the past.

A significant difference between carbide and steel blades is that each carbide tooth is individually brazed onto a strong, flexible spring-steel blade back. In fact, the recommended tension for a carbide blade is almost twice that of carbon steel, giving carbide blades much greater beam strength. The carbide teeth are precisely ground on the face, top, and both sides, which results in truer, more precise cuts.

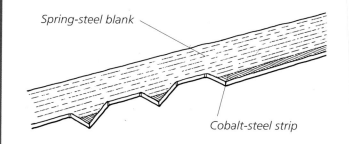

How a Bimetal Blade Is Made

A strip of cobalt steel is welded onto a spring-steel blank before the teeth are cut. When the teeth are cut, all that remains of the cobalt steel is the tooth tip.

Spring-steel blank

Cobalt-steel strip

A carbide-tipped blade is economical because it stays sharp for so long.

As you would expect, carbide bandsaw blades are significantly more expensive than ordinary carbon-steel blades. However, a carbide blade will typically outlast carbon steel 25 to 1, and carbide can be resharpened. Although more expensive initially, carbide blades are much more economical than carbon-steel blades. This is especially true for resawing.

Stellite

Stellite is the brand name of a unique type of carbide that is reportedly better suited for woodworking applications. Stellite isn't as hard as regular carbide, but it's not as brittle either. This gives Stellite the advantage of greater shock resistance. Like carbide, Stellite promises longer wear and better-quality cuts.

In many other ways, Stellite blades are a lot like carbide blades. The Stellite teeth are brazed onto the blade body, then precisely ground. And like carbide blades, Stellite blades are expensive.

Blade Width and Thickness

Thickness is related to width. Take a look at a manufacturer's blade catalog and you'll see that as blades get wider, the steel used for the blade gets thicker. This is standard industry practice, and it gives wider blades greater beam strength and stiffness. Because of the additional stiffness, wider blades need more force to reach the recommended tension, which means that they should be used only on bandsaws with frames strong enough to provide the necessary tension. Also, wide blades have a minimum wheel diameter that they can flex around without breaking.

The width of a blade relates to its beam strength. Beam strength refers to the fact that a bandsaw blade supported between two sets of guides acts like a beam when the workpiece is fed into the blade. Like a beam, the wider the blade, the stiffer it will be. Several factors can reduce the beam strength of a blade. If the blade is dull, if the workpiece is very thick, if there is insufficient tension, if the feed rate is too great, or if the blade has the wrong type of teeth for a job, the blade will be more likely to bend (see the drawing on

---

Beam Strength

A bandsaw blade bows when the beam strength isn't great enough to resist the feed pressure.

Feed pressure

The front of the blade is in compression, while the back is in tension.

Bigger isn't better

Don't try to use a blade wider or thicker than your saw can tension. Cranking up to accommodate a heavy blade can bend your saw's frame, as well as damage wheels, shafts, and bearings.

the facing page). Increasing the blade tension or blade width will increase the beam strength.

Attempting to exceed the maximum blade width for your bandsaw can wreck the saw. As you tension a blade that's too wide for the saw, the stress can distort the frame, possibly beyond repair. The excessive tension also places potentially damaging forces on the saw's wheels, shafts, and bearings.

Tooth Form

Tooth form refers to the design of the tooth and gullet, specifically the tooth size, shape, and rake angle. The three commonly known blade forms for cutting wood are the regular, skip, and hook. Another form that is gaining in popularity is the variable tooth.

> **Tooth form is vital**
> More than any other factor, the tooth form determines how well a blade will cut in a given situation.

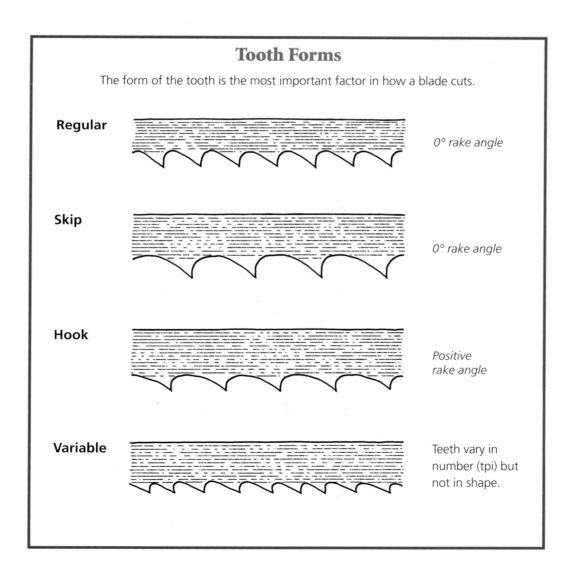

Tooth Forms

The form of the tooth is the most important factor in how a blade cuts.

Regular — 0° rake angle

Skip — 0° rake angle

Hook — Positive rake angle

Variable — Teeth vary in number (tpi) but not in shape.

Tooth Forms and Their Uses

Tooth form	Number of teeth	Rake angle	Gullet	Best uses	Limitations
Regular	Many teeth, evenly spaced	0°, scraping action cuts cleanly	Small	• Precise cutting of curves	• Gullets fill with sawdust quickly, heating blade • Requires slow feed rate
Skip	Fewer than regular; every other tooth is missing	0°, scraping action cuts cleanly	Large	• Resawing, ripping thick stock	• Doesn't cut as smoothly as regular-tooth blades
Hook	Similar to skip	Positive rake angle, aggressive cut	Large	• Aggressive blade allows a faster feed rate • Good for resawing and ripping, especially in hardwoods	• Same as skip
Variable	Both many and few in sections on the same blade; vary in size but not in shape	Can have either 0° or a positive rake angle	Like teeth: large or small, varying in size but not in shape	• Much less vibration; makes for a very smooth cut • Moderate feed rate	• Expensive

Regular tooth

The regular-tooth form, sometimes called the standard form, has evenly spaced teeth for smooth, precise cutting. Teeth and gullets are the same size, and the rake, or cutting angle, is 0°. Compared to other tooth forms, regular blades have more teeth, and the 0° cutting angle scrapes the wood surface clean. This combination of features leaves a smooth surface. Regular-tooth blades are a great choice for sawing curves.

The disadvantage of regular-tooth blades is that the gullets are too small to effectively cut thick stock. Remember that the purpose of the gullets is to haul away the sawdust from the kerf. If you attempt to cut thick stock with a regular blade, the gullets become full before the teeth exit the stock, thus cutting slows down and the teeth overheat. Obviously, regular blades are not designed for fast cutting. In fact, if you push the stock too hard in an effort to increase the cutting rate, the cut actually slows down as the gullets become packed with sawdust.

Skip tooth

As you might assess from the name, the skip form "skips" every other tooth. Skip-tooth blades have fewer teeth and larger gullets than regular-tooth blades. The large gullets can efficiently carry the saw-dust away from the kerf. This makes skip-tooth blades fast cutting. Like regular-tooth blades, skip-tooth blades also have a 0° rake angle that scrapes the wood away cleanly. But because they have fewer teeth, skip-tooth blades don't cut as smoothly as regular blades.

Skip blades are best suited for resawing and ripping thick stock. They also work well for cutting softwoods. The only problem with skip-tooth blades is that the more efficient hook-tooth blade has outmoded them. Why do manufacturers still produce skip blades? One sawblade manufacturer to whom I spoke said his company still makes skip-tooth blades mainly because it's difficult to convince people to change—short of sending people a free hook blade to try.

Hook tooth

The hook tooth is really a further development of the skip tooth. The hook form has large gullets and teeth like that of skip blades, but the teeth have a positive rake angle that makes them cut more aggressively. Because of that aggressive nature, hook blades have less feed resistance than skip blades. In fact, they almost seem to feed themselves. Hook-tooth blades are a great choice for resawing and ripping thick stock.

Variable tooth

The variable-tooth blade is a hybrid among bandsaw blades. Variable-tooth blades can have regular teeth with a 0° rake angle or a more aggressive positive rake angle. But the unique feature of this type of blade is that the tooth size and spacing vary on the same blade. This means that both the teeth and gullets vary in size but not in shape. The unique design dramatically reduces vibration; the result is a quieter blade and a very smooth cut.

To understand how this works, it's helpful to think of a bandsaw blade as a string on a musical instrument (a fiddle if you like country music or a violin if you prefer classical). Both the strings on an instrument and on a bandsaw blade are under tension, but for different reasons. You want a string on an instrument to vibrate in order to produce a sound. This is called harmonic vibration. But you want to limit vibration on a bandsaw blade because vibrations create a rough

Tooth Set

Bandsaw blades designed for woodworking have an alternate set pattern. Every tooth is set in an alternating sequence.

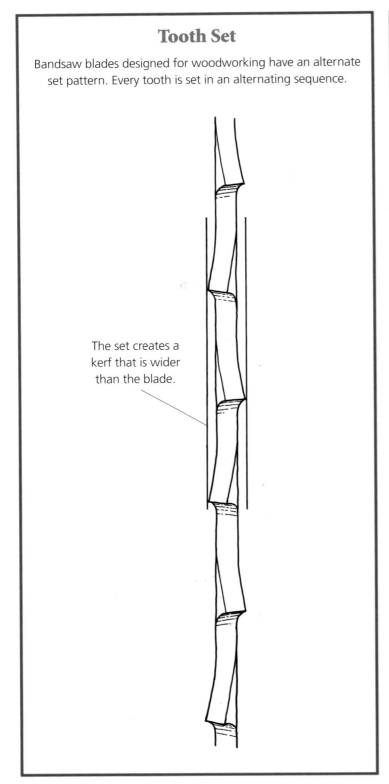

The set creates a kerf that is wider than the blade.

surface on the stock. By varying the tooth and gullet size, you effectively limit the vibrations and create a smoother surface.

Tooth set

Tooth set is the bending of the teeth left and right to create a kerf wider than the blade body. This is important to prevent binding during cutting. There are several set patterns available, but most are designed for metal cutting. Alternate set is really the only style that is effective for woodworking blades. With alternate set, every other tooth is bent in the same direction, left, right, and so on (see the drawing at left).

Although carbide teeth are not bent, they are wider than the steel body to which they're brazed. Then they're ground to create a set pattern that helps keep the blade running true.

Pitch

Pitch is simply the number of teeth per inch (tpi) on a blade length measured from the tips of the teeth. Pitch determines two factors: the speed at which the blade will cut through the stock and the smoothness of the cut surface.

Blades with a fine pitch have more teeth per inch of blade length than those with a coarse pitch. A greater number of teeth means that each tooth is small and thus takes a small bite that leaves the surface smooth. A greater number of teeth also reduces the size of the gullets. Since small gullets can't haul away dust very quickly, fine-pitch blades cut slower and tend to get hotter than coarser blades.

The opposite is true for coarse-pitch blades. Both the teeth and the gullets are larger, so each tooth bites off a greater amount of wood, and the large gullets can easily remove the sawdust from the kerf.

Choosing a Blade

Getting the results you expect from your bandsaw greatly depends on having the best blade for the job at hand. In my own shop, I keep an assortment of blades so I'm always ready for the next woodworking project.

Thumbing through the pages of an industrial bandsaw blade catalog can seem very confusing. You should realize, though, that you can eliminate many of the blades listed simply because they are

Coarser is usually better

In most cutting situations, I choose coarser-pitched blades over fine. The gullets on fine-pitched blades get full of sawdust, and cutting slows dramatically. At the same time, the tips of the teeth get hot, and on a carbon-steel blade they easily become overheated and dull.

designed for cutting various metals. Rather than looking at what blades are available, I find it's much easier to narrow down the blade choices based upon the types of cuts I'll be making (see the sidebar on pp. 70-71). Below is a list of the cuts I make in my own shop:

- Curves in furniture parts such as legs, feet, and skirts. This category also includes compound curves.

- Intricate scrollwork such as the tiny curves found on mirrors and small, detailed boxes.

- Resawing 1-in.-thick soft poplar or pine into thin stock for drawer parts or other small projects.

- Ripping thick, heavy hardwood into rough sizes before milling.

- Slicing veneer from wide, highly figured hardwood stock.

- Cutting joints on furniture parts.

- Sawing small, figured logs into planks for drying.

For every job, it's important to consider the blade width, pitch, and tooth form.

Which Blade Should I Use?

Choosing a blade can be confusing until you're familiar with all the factors. Here are some examples to get you started.

This 2-pitch bimetal blade makes quick work of poplar.

Resawing 6-in.-wide poplar for drawer parts

Option 1: Carbide-tipped, 3 pitch, hook tooth.

Option 2: Bimetal, 2 pitch, hook tooth.

Comments: Poplar is soft and cuts easily. The bimetal blade would be less expensive, but the carbide blade would last much longer. For greatest beam strength, use the widest blade that your bandsaw can properly tension.

Slicing ¹⁄₁₆-in. veneer from a 9-in.-wide crotch-walnut plank

Option 1: Carbide-tipped, 2/3 variable pitch, hook tooth.

Option 2: Spring steel, 3/4 variable pitch, hook tooth.

Option 3: Carbide-tipped, 3 pitch, hook tooth.

Option 4: Bimetal, 3 pitch, hook tooth.

Comments: Walnut crotch has dramatic figure and is expensive—when you can find it. I try to get as much veneer as I possibly can from a valuable plank like this. A carbon blade would be my last choice

A variable-pitch carbide-tipped blade is a great choice for accurately sawing veneer.

Ripping hardwoods on the bandsaw is easy with a ½-in.-wide, 4-pitch blade.

because it dulls quickly. The variable-pitch carbide blade is very expensive, but the cut is incredibly smooth. Both of the carbide blades are stiff and require a strong frame to properly tension. The spring-steel variable-pitch blade is an excellent choice, particularly for saws with wheel diameters less than 18 in. It tensions easily since it's only 0.022 in. thick. This blade cuts incredibly smoothly, and it's relatively inexpensive compared to carbide blades—although you can't expect it to last as long. Best of all, the kerf from this blade is a slim $\frac{1}{32}$ in., half that of the other blades in this category. You'll definitely get more veneer from this blade.

Ripping 2-in.-thick hardwood

Option 1: Carbide-tipped, 4 pitch, hook tooth, $\frac{1}{2}$ in. wide.

Option 2: Carbon steel, 4 pitch, hook tooth, $\frac{1}{2}$ in. or $\frac{3}{4}$ in. wide.

Comments: If you have a 14-in. bandsaw, you'll probably get truer cuts with a $\frac{1}{2}$-in.-wide, 0.025-in.-thick blade rather than a $\frac{3}{4}$-in.-wide, 0.032-in.-thick blade. Your saw stands a better chance of tensioning the thinner blade.

Cutting contours in $\frac{7}{8}$-in.-thick maple (minimum radius $\frac{9}{16}$ in.)

Option 1: Bimetal, 10 pitch, regular tooth, $\frac{1}{4}$ in. wide.

Option 2: Bimetal, 6 pitch, regular tooth, $\frac{1}{4}$ in. wide.

Comments: The 10-pitch blade would create a smoother surface, thus requiring less cleanup of sawmarks.

Cutting scrolls in $\frac{1}{4}$-in. hardwood (minimum radius $\frac{1}{16}$ in.)

Blade: Bimetal, 24 pitch, regular tooth, $\frac{1}{16}$ in. wide.

Comments: This tiny $\frac{1}{16}$-in. blade is your only choice for cutting tight contours. You'll need to replace the steel guide blocks with hardwood blocks or Cool Blocks. This blade can't be used on bandsaws equipped with bearing guides.

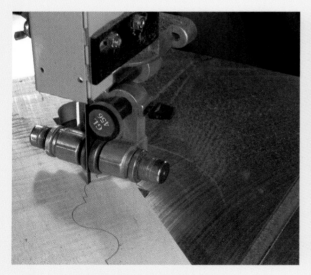

A $\frac{1}{4}$-in., 6-pitch blade is a good choice for cutting most contours, but a 10-pitch blade leaves a smoother surface.

A $\frac{1}{16}$-in., 24-pitch blade cuts intricate scrolls with little or no cleanup required.

My Favorite Bandsaw Blades

Here is a list of the blades that I keep on hand.

Carbide-tipped, 2/3 pitch, variable tooth, 1¼ in.

I use this stiff blade for slicing veneer from premium, highly figured planks. Because of the 0.042-in. thickness of the blade body, you'll need at least a 24-in. bandsaw to run this blade. Its recommended tension is 25,000 psi.

If you own a 14-in. saw, a ½-in. by 0.025-in., 3-pitch, hook-tooth, carbide-tipped blade is a great choice. Most 24-in. bandsaws can tension such a wide blade. You'll be impressed with the remarkably smooth surfaces it produces. Although this blade is expensive, the carbide teeth will outlast a carbon-steel blade by 25 to 1.

Spring steel, variable tooth, ½ in.

The main advantage of this blade is the tiny $\frac{1}{32}$-in. kerf. Designed especially for resawing, this spring-steel blade is marketed under the trade name The Wood Slicer. Although it doesn't come close to the long life of a carbide-tipped blade, it cuts almost as smoothly. The thin kerf means you can squeeze every slice of veneer possible out of your next prized board.

Bimetal, 3 pitch, hook tooth, ½ in.

The high-speed steel teeth in a bimetal blade stay sharp much longer than those of carbon steel, yet the price is only two to three times higher. This blade will never approach the smoothness of a carbide blade, but I use this one as a general-purpose resawing blade and save the carbide for cutting veneer.

Carbon-steel blades, various pitches, regular tooth, ⅛ in., ¼ in., and ⅜ in.

These three blades handle all my contour cutting. I choose the pitch based upon the stock thickness.

Width is determined by the type of cut—whether you're sawing a straight line or a curve. Tooth pitch is determined by the stock thickness. Tooth form influences how aggressively or smoothly the blade will cut. I always begin by selecting the blade width.

Selecting the best width

Each blade width has a minimum radius that it can cut without binding and dragging through the kerf. Attempting to squeeze a blade through a turn that is too tight can result in a number of problems. The blade will break, the teeth will be twisted into the guides (which causes them to lose sharpness and set), or the blade will be pulled off the saw's wheels. And anytime a blade comes off the wheels while the saw is running there's a good possibility that the teeth will be damaged or the blade will bend into something that resembles modern art.

The blade-radius chart on p. 74 shows the minimum radius that each width of blade can turn. Such a chart can often be found on the box that a blade is packed in when shipped. You may find it helpful to post a copy of this chart in a conspicuous place, such as on the wheel cover of your bandsaw or on the wall where you store blades.

You may be wondering why you just can't mount a narrow blade (such as ¼ in.) on your saw and cut all curves with that. This does work—but only to a degree. Narrow blades have a tendency

Factors to Consider When Selecting a Blade

Blade thickness

Less than 0.025 in. to save material when resawing

0.025 in. for wheel diameters no less than 12 in.

0.032 in. for wheel diameters no less than 18 in.

0.035 in. for wheel diameters no less than 24 in.

Tooth material

Carbon steel is inexpensive and readily available with a variety of characteristics.
Use carbide for resawing; it has long blade life and gives the smoothest finished surface.
Use bimetal for heavy ripping.

Blade width	Best use
¹⁄₁₆ in. to ⅛ in.	Scrolling
³⁄₁₆ in. to ½ in.	Cutting curves
⅜ in. to 1 in. and above	Resawing (base your selection on what your saw can tension)

Pitch

2/3 tpi	Resawing
3 tpi	Resawing and ripping thick stock
4 tpi	Ripping stock 1½ in. to 3 in. thick
6 tpi	General ripping and cutting curves in stock more than 1 in. thick
10 tpi	Cutting curves in stock ¾ in. to 1 in. thick
14 tpi	Cutting curves in stock ½ in. to ¾ in. thick
18 tpi	Scrolling in stock ⅜ in. to ⅝ in. thick
24 tpi	Scrolling in stock ¼ in. to ½ in. thick

Tooth form

Regular	Curves and scrolls
Variable	Resawing veneer and other valuable stock
Hook	Ripping and resawing

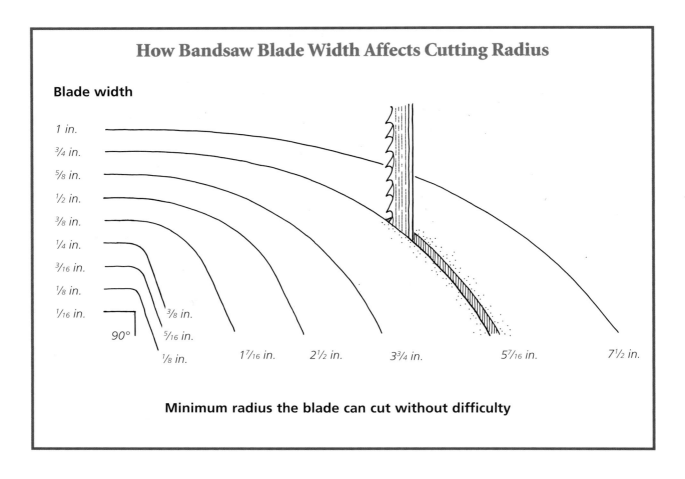

How Bandsaw Blade Width Affects Cutting Radius

Blade width

1 in.
3/4 in.
5/8 in.
1/2 in.
3/8 in.
1/4 in.
3/16 in.
1/8 in.
1/16 in.

90°

3/8 in.
5/16 in.
1/8 in.   1 7/16 in.   2 1/2 in.   3 3/4 in.   5 7/16 in.   7 1/2 in.

Minimum radius the blade can cut without difficulty

Use the widest blade

Use the widest blade possible for any job—even when cutting curves. Wider blades wander less and produce smoother curves. The limiting factor on blade width is your saw's ability to tension a blade. Many consumer-grade saws cannot tension a blade any wider than ½ in.

to wander. If you try to cut a large radius, such as a 36-in.-dia. tabletop for example, you'll have a hard time keeping the blades from straying from the line. You'll cut more precisely with a 1-in.-wide blade. However, with practice you'll probably cut a majority of curved work with a ¼-in. or ⅜-in. blade.

When resawing, it's always an advantage to use the widest blade that your bandsaw can properly tension. Keep in

mind that the widest blade a saw can tension may not be as wide as the widest blade it can accept. For smaller saws, you'll most likely get better results from the next size narrower blade. Wider blades have more beam strength, but to fully create the beam strength the blade must be properly tensioned.

My own bandsaw, a 24-in. machine, can tension a 1¼-in. by 0.042-in. carbide blade to 25,000 psi. This blade is my best option for resawing thick, valuable stock because of its tremendous beam strength. With this blade I can easily slice 12-in.-wide boards into veneer that is consistently ¹⁄₃₂ in. thick.

Many of the consumer bandsaws that are mounted on a stand will accept a ¾-in. by 0.032-in. blade. This is your best choice for resawing if your saw can provide the tension it requires. If you experience blade deflection and a loss of quality in the cut with the ¾-in. blade, you'd be better off with a ½-in. by 0.025-in. blade.

Selecting the best tooth form

Tooth form affects the performance of the blade more than any other factor. A regular tooth gives the smoothest cut; a hook tooth cuts aggressively with little feed resistance; and a variable pitch cuts both smoothly and aggressively.

For cutting contours, a regular-tooth blade is often the best choice because it has the greatest number of teeth. This combined with a 0° rake angle gives you a smooth, finished surface that requires little cleanup.

A hook tooth is my choice for general resawing, such as when sawing thick planks into thin drawer parts. The coarser pitch combined with a positive cutting angle makes quick work of any hardwood.

When sawing veneer from a plank of valuable hardwood, a hook blade will do a great job, but a variable-pitch blade will leave a smoother finish. Also remember that the variable-pitch blade reduces vibration during cutting.

Selecting the proper pitch

Pitch is the number of teeth measured from tooth tip to tooth tip on 1 in. of blade length. Blades with a continuous pattern of teeth are called constant pitch.

Blades with teeth that vary in size are called variable pitch.

The major factor to consider when selecting proper tooth pitch is the thickness of the stock. In general, you want to select a blade that will have no less than 6 and no more than 12 teeth in the stock at any given time (see the drawing on p. 76). For example, if you're cutting 1-in.-thick stock, a 6-pitch blade would be a good choice, but a 14-pitch one would be too fine. However, if the stock were only ½ in. thick, a 14-pitch blade would be optimum for the stock thickness. Selecting the proper pitch is made easier by the fact that there is a limited number of pitch selections for each blade width. Although the range of available pitch is broad, from 2 tpi to 32 tpi, wide blades generally have fewer teeth and narrow blades have a greater number of teeth.

It's also important to consider how pitch will affect the life of the blade, specifically a carbon-steel blade that is easily damaged by overheating. For example, a fine-pitch blade will overheat when used on thick stock because the gullets become packed with sawdust. This causes the blade to quickly dull and lose its set. Once this occurs, the blade is worthless, so choosing the correct pitch will substantially increase blade life.

Remember that the blade pitch determines the smoothness of the cut and the speed at which the stock can be cut.

> ### Try a narrower resaw blade
>
> If you have a 14-in. bandsaw, try resawing with a ⅜-in. or ½-in. variable-pitch blade. Most saws have sufficient stiffness to tension these blades, which cut fairly aggressively and leave a wonderfully smooth surface.

Selecting the Best Pitch

You'll get the best cuts when there are between 6 and 12 teeth in the stock (center).
The cut is smooth and because the sawdust is rapidly carried away, the feed rate can be faster.

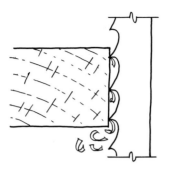

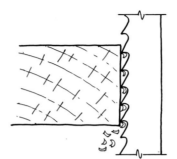

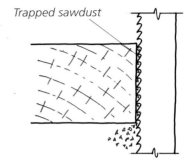

Trapped sawdust

Fewer than 6 teeth in the stock can cause vibration and a rough cut.

With more than 12 teeth in the stock, the small gullets fill with sawdust and the blade overheats.

Feed slowly

When bandsawing, slower cuts are usually best, whether you're resawing or cutting contours. You'll get a cleaner cut, and you can saw closer to the line.

Speed is most important in a production setting and when ripping rough stock. However, the average woodworker normally isn't cutting enough material to be concerned about whether the blade is cutting 20 ft. per minute or 22 ft. When sawing veneer, a slow feed rate gives you a truer cut and a smoother finish with less cleanup of sawmarks—and maybe even an extra slice of veneer from your plank.

When cutting contours, you'll be able to follow the layout line more precisely if you don't hurry while cutting. The advantage is that you'll spend less time later removing bumps and irregularities where the blade didn't quite follow the line.

Sometimes smoothness and precision may not be too important. When I'm sawing a contour that will later be flush-trimmed with a router or a shaper, I'm not concerned with the surface quality from the bandsaw. In a situation such as this, I'm using the bandsaw merely to remove the excess wood before shaping.

However, when cutting fine, detailed scrollwork, I am concerned with surface quality. Some details are so fine it is difficult or impossible to smooth them afterwards with a file or other tool. In this case, I want the blade to create a smooth, finished surface, so I use a slow, steady feed so I can carefully follow the line.

You must decide which is more important to you—speed or smoothness. You can't get the best of both in the same blade. However, you can select a blade that is a good compromise.

Caring for Your Blades

The heat generated from sawing causes pitch and gum to build up on the surfaces of the teeth and in the gullets. Once the teeth and gullets become covered with gunk, the blade performs as though it were dull. Buildup can occur quickly with resinous woods like pine, but all woods contribute to the problem. The excessive heat from a blade with too fine a pitch significantly speeds up the accumulation of crud, so selecting the proper pitch helps with this problem.

Cleaning blades is easy, and for the small amount of effort it takes, you get a substantial difference in blade performance. Most woodworking stores and catalogs sell a blade-cleaning liquid. To use it, you simply remove the blade, spray it with cleaner, and wipe off the residue.

Because bandsaw-blade teeth can be easily damaged, I always store my blades on a wall-mounted rack so the teeth don't touch. Carbide teeth are brittle and especially fragile.

Have you noticed how blades are coiled into three loops when you purchase them? Coiling the blades is easy to do, and the blades take up a lot less room in your shop. There are three ways to coil a blade (see the photo essay on pp. 78-79). Try all three to find the one that you like best.

Cleaning the pitch from this blade will dramatically improve its performance.

WOOD PITCH CLEANER

FOR WOOD CUTTING TOOLS

LENOX

Coiling Blades for Storage

There are three standard ways to coil a bandsaw blade. Try each one to see which is best for you.

First Method

1 Grasp the blade with both hands in the middle of the blade (photo at right). Your palms should be facing inward, leading with your thumbs on the outside of the blade.

2 Twist the blade inward with your thumbs, and as you do so, bring your hands closer together (photo at left below).

3 As you bring your hands together, three coils will form (photo at right below).

Second Method

1 Grasp the blade with both hands in the middle of the blade.

2 Twist the blade forward with your right hand and backward with your left. The blade will coil into three rings.

Third Method

1 Grasp the blade with one hand with your fingers facing toward you, and allow the blade to rest on the floor (with a wide blade, you may need to use two hands). Place your foot on the blade to hold it in place.

2 Rotate your wrist, and as you do so, push the twisting blade toward the floor. This will cause the blade to coil into three rings.

Uncoiling a large blade can be tricky. By simply grasping two of the coils and spreading them apart, the blade will naturally uncoil, but be careful. A large, coiled blade has a lot of tension in it, and if it suddenly springs open you can get a nasty cut. I recommend wearing gloves and safety glasses and holding the blade at arm's length when you uncoil it.

A resistance welder makes welding bandsaw blades almost foolproof. It's the fastest way to make your own bandsaw blades.

Making Your Own Carbon-Steel Blades

If you have the time and the inclination, you can save money by welding your own carbon-steel blades from coil stock. By purchasing the stock in 100-ft. rolls, then cutting and welding or brazing the blades yourself, you can expect to pay about half of what you normally spend on blades.

I recommend welding only carbon-steel blades that are ½ in. or less in width. The spring steel used in the bodies of bimetal and carbide blades is very difficult to weld properly. Welding them is best left to professional saw shops.

Once you've learned to weld blades, you'll find it comes in handy. If a blade breaks before it's dull, you can fix it yourself. Also, you may occasionally want to make an interior cut on stock that's too thick for a jigsaw. You can thread the blade through a hole in the stock, weld the blade ends together, and make the cut with your bandsaw.

There are two ways you can weld a blade in your own shop. You can buy a resistance welder that's similar to the one saw shops use, or you can braze the blades with a torch and silver brazing solder.

The first method, using a resistance welder, is faster but the welder is an expensive purchase. On the other hand, you can buy an inexpensive brazing kit from most woodworking-supply outfits, but brazing is time-consuming and has more of a learning curve. In the next section, I'll outline the steps involved in using both of these methods.

Resistance welding

A resistance welder uses electrical energy to create intense heat to fuse the blade ends together. The welding process leaves the joint brittle, so it must be annealed by being reheated and cooled slowly. Here's how to weld a blade with a resistance welder.

1. Cut the blade to length. Most bandsaws will accept blades that are 1 in. or so longer than the specified length. I always cut a new blade the maximum length the saw will accept. This gives me an extra try at welding if the first attempt fails.

2. Check the ends of the cut for squareness. If they are not 90°, use a grinder to make them so.

3. Clamp the blade ends within the electrodes of the welder. The ends of the blade should touch.

4. Set the pressure control. The setting is determined by the width of the blade.

5. Press the weld button. Hold the button until the weld is complete. During welding, the blade ends will turn bright orange and quickly return to normal color at the completion of the weld. The entire process takes three or four seconds.

6. Annealing. Reposition the blade at the front edge of the electrode clamp, then jog the annealing button until the steel at the weld is cherry red in color.

Safety Guidelines for Using a Resistance Welder

- Wear eye protection when welding and grinding blades.
- Don't touch the electrode jaws when welding.
- Avoid touching the blade ends. All three steps of this procedure—welding, annealing, and grinding—heat the steel enough to cause a serious burn.

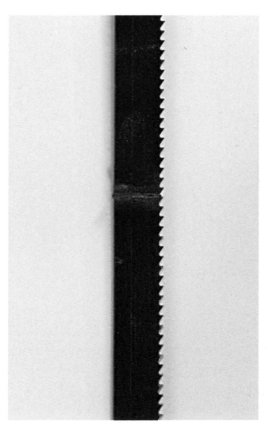

This is how the joint appears after resistance welding. The excess flash must be ground away so the blade runs smoothly over the wheels and through the guides.

Troubleshooting Welding Problems

If you've never used a resistance blade welder, then you may be one of the lucky ones who get it right the very first time. If not, I've provided a list of problems along with their solutions that you can use as a guide to get it right.

Problem	Diagnosis
There's a spark but no weld when the weld button is depressed.	• The ends of the blade are not square and even. • The pressure switch is set too low.
The joint is melted with a large gap or gaps in the weld.	• The pressure switch is set too high.
The blade easily breaks before you can even mount it on the bandsaw.	• The blade was overheated during annealing.
The blade ends are overlapped.	• The ends must be flat and straight so that they butt together perfectly when clamped in the electrode jaws.
Excessive flash on narrow blades.	• The pressure switch is set too high. • The first tooth on each end of a regular-tooth blade should be ground away before welding.

Allow a few minutes for the blade to cool naturally.

7. Grinding the flash. Once you've annealed the weld, grind away the flash around the joint so that the blade will run smoothly through the saw guides. Be careful not to grind the blade or teeth; grinding into the blade body weakens it. Also, grind the flash away slowly so you don't overheat the blade.

8. Final annealing. After grinding, anneal the blade once more, then allow the blade to cool for a few minutes before using it.

Brazing

Brazing is a much more economical option for making blades than using a resistance welder. Most woodworking-supply houses offer brazing kits that con-

To braze a blade, the ends must be held firmly in position. Apply flux to the joint before brazing.

tain a blade fixture for holding the end while brazing, a jar of flux, and silver brazing alloy for less than $50. You'll have to supply a torch that burns propane, butane, or MAPP gas. A torch with a small head makes it easier for you to avoid overheating the joint.

When properly done, a brazed joint is actually stronger than the blade itself. In fact, brazing is used for several other woodworking applications, such as joining carbide sawteeth to blade bodies and joining carbide cutting surfaces to router bits. Here are the steps I use to braze a bandsaw blade.

1. Bevel the blade ends. For greatest strength, the ends of the blade must be filed or ground to a bevel. The width of the bevel should be three times the blade thickness, and the ends of the bevel must be 90°. To ensure a uniform bevel, you'll need to clamp the blade ends. I use a piece of angle iron held in a vise and bulldog clips to hold the blade to the angle iron.

2. Clean the blade ends. Remove any trace of a burr from filing or grinding, then clean the blade ends with mineral spirits to remove any oil that may prevent the alloy from flowing. Afterwards, wipe the ends dry.

3. Clamp the blade ends in the fixture. Proper alignment is crucial for a strong braze. The bevels should overlap, and the backs should be flush.

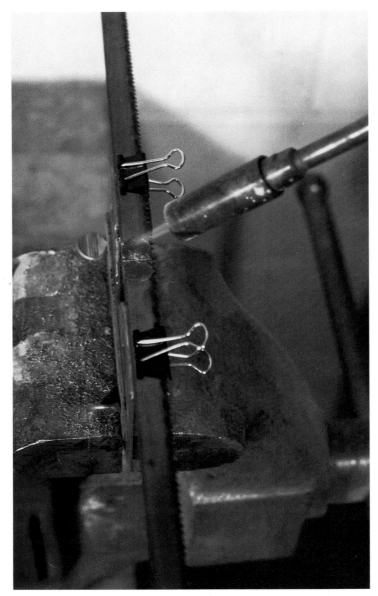

The blade is heated with a small torch until the edges are a dull red.

4. Spread the flux. Spread the flux about ½ in. up from the blade ends. It's important to get flux on the bevels as well. To do this, I push the lower bevel downward, which allows me to get the bristles of the flux brush into the joint.

5. Brazing. This is the most difficult part of the procedure. The goal is to evenly heat the blade ends to the point that the alloy flows into the joint. The flux and the blade ends provide an indication of when you've reached the proper temperature. When the temperature is right, the flux will be clear, the blade will be almost white, and the edges will be a dull red. Next, place the end of the alloy onto the joint while continuing to apply heat with the torch. As the alloy is touched to the hot steel, it will be drawn into the joint by capillary action and create a strong bond.

7. Remove excess alloy. After allowing the blade to cool, remove any excess alloy from the joint. First, clean off the flux with a rag, then smooth the joint with a mill file, being careful not to dull the teeth.

Safety

The bandsaw has a reputation as being a benign machine. The back of the blade can't cut you like a circular sawblade can. More important, you won't experience violent kickbacks while using your bandsaw. But any power tool that is designed for cutting wood can quickly and easily wreak havoc with flesh and bone. I learned early in my woodworking career to treat the bandsaw with the respect that it deserves.

When I work on any machine, I follow all the safety rules. Most woodworking accidents occur because the operator did some procedure he knew he shouldn't have done. By requiring myself and my students to adhere to the rules in every situation, no matter how small the cut, I've managed to build furniture and teach a shopful of students for more than 20 years with no serious injuries.

A turning blade is an obvious safety hazard, but bandsaws also produce a more insidious hazard—dust. It's essential to protect your respiratory system from the dust, and the best way to do that is with a dust-collection system. There's no need to worry about complicated separators and ductwork: A shop vac is an adequate bandsaw dust-collection system when coupled with a mask.

Bandsaw Safety Guidelines

When it comes to bandsaw safety, you, the operator, play the critical role. I've found that by keeping my bandsaw and its guards in working order and following a few simple guidelines, bandsaw safety is virtually assured. The guidelines that I use are listed on the next two pages.

The Bandsaw Won't Kick Back

Because the blade on a bandsaw is moving downward as it passes through the workpiece, there is no force to do anything other than hold the work down.

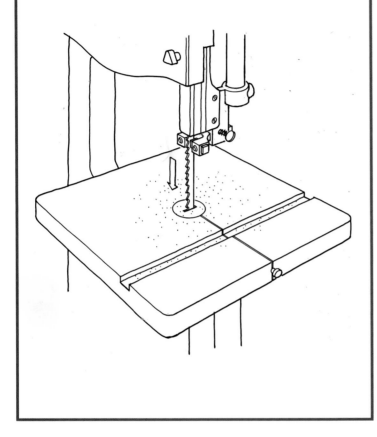

Keep your fingers out of the path of the blade. Although this may seem obvious, it's easy to allow your fingers to be in the wrong place as you are cutting contours. As you turn and rotate the workpiece to follow the layout line, you must frequently reposition your hands to keep them a safe distance from the blade's path. I never allow the sawing operation to prevent me from being aware of my hand position.

Gradually decrease the feed pressure as you approach the end of the cut. As the blade nears the edge of the workpiece, be ready for the fact that the feed resistance is dramatically reduced right at the end of the cut. If you continue pushing the workpiece with the same degree of force, you can lose control as the blade exits the kerf.

Use push sticks when ripping narrow stock or when resawing. Keep your fingers intact by keeping them a safe distance from the blade. I keep a push stick in a convenient location and use it when ripping narrow stock or when resawing. It's impossible to push the stock safely with your hands during the last few inches of resawing. The stock is often too thin for safe placement of your hands. Also, I've seen the last few inches suddenly and unexpectedly split apart when resawing. I always place a push block within easy reach, and I use it to finish the cut.

Always keep the wheel covers shut while the bandsaw is running. It may be tempting to check the tracking or guide adjustment while the saw is running, but if the tracking is way off and the blade jumps the wheels or breaks, you are unprotected.

Keep the upper guide adjusted approximately ¼ in. above the stock. One of the most common bandsaw safety mistakes is to cut a thick piece of stock and then cut a thinner piece without first lowering the guide (see the top photo on p. 88). If you don't lower the guide, a long length of blade is exposed, and it's more likely the blade will deflect while cutting, possibly ruining your cut.

Keep the blade guard in place. The guidepost has a sheet-metal guard to cover the blade. If the blade breaks, the guard is one of your major lines of defense. If you must remove the guard for blade changing, always replace it.

Disconnect the bandsaw from its power source before changing blades. I also make all tracking and guide adjustments with the power disconnected.

Always wear eye and ear protection when operating a bandsaw. Today more than ever, there's a broad selection of safety equipment from which to choose. It's easy to find eye and ear protection that's lightweight, comfortable, and effective, so make use of it.

Wear gloves when handling large blades. Long, wide blades have a lot of tension when coiled. When uncoiling a large blade (or any blade, for that matter) wear gloves and use caution.

Protect your respiratory system. The dust that's generated from the bandsaw is some of the finest from any woodworking machine. And it's the fine dust that does the most damage to your lungs. Also, fine dust stays suspended in the shop air for a long time. For these reasons, I use a dust

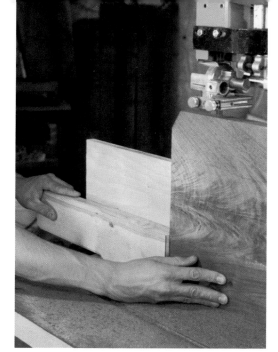

It's not uncommon for the last couple of inches of a board being resawn to suddenly split. A simple push block keeps your hands out of danger. Note that the hand on the board is behind the blade.

What to Do If a Blade Breaks

Ideally, blades don't break or if they do, the teeth are already worn out and it's time to throw out the blade anyway. But blades do occasionally break prematurely because of excess tension or stress from trying to push the blade through too tight a turn.

When a blade does break, it typically stays safely enclosed within the saw cabinet. When this happens, use the foot brake (if your saw has one) to stop the lower wheel. Of course, the brake doesn't stop the upper wheel unless the blade is intact, which it isn't. So for safety's sake, don't open the cabinet to install a new blade until both wheels have come to a complete stop. Otherwise the spinning top wheel could potentially send the blade or a fragment of it flying.

collector with my bandsaw, especially when resawing, which produces a huge amount of dust. Because bandsaw dust is so fine, you'll want a collector that traps fine dust and not just chips.

Keeping the upper guides about ¼ in. above the cut minimizes blade exposure.

Fitting Dust Collection to Your Bandsaw

Fine wood dust stays airborne the longest and does the most damage to your health. That's exactly the kind of dust a bandsaw produces, and lots of it, when resawing. Luckily, it's not difficult to add dust collection to your bandsaw—and you won't need an expensive collector, either. Any shop vacuum cleaner will do the job (but wear your hearing protection because the average shop vac is incredibly loud).

The most important feature of any dust-collection system is the ability to trap the fine dust particles. Many dust collectors, portable or otherwise, really only trap and hold large particles such as wood chips and shavings. The systems I've been most impressed with use a pleated filter to

Protect your lungs

Even the best collector can't capture 100% of the dust, so it's still a good idea to wear a high-quality dust mask.

Bandsaw Safety Guidelines

Here's a list of bandsaw safety guidelines. Photocopy it and hang it in your shop.

- Keep your fingers out of the path of the blade.
- Decrease the feed pressure as you near the end of a cut.
- Use push sticks when ripping or resawing.
- Keep the wheel covers shut when the saw is running.
- Keep the upper guide about ¼ in. above the workpiece.
- Keep the blade guard in place.
- Disconnect the bandsaw power source before changing blades.
- Wear eye and ear protection when bandsawing.
- Wear gloves when handling blades.
- Protect your respiratory system.

This dust collection fitting is directly beneath the table to catch the dust at the source.

trap the fine, flourlike dust. This filter resembles the filters used in your car's air and oil systems.

Unlike bandsaws made 20 years ago, most new bandsaws have a dust-collection fitting. Most are mounted directly beneath the saw's table, near the lower guide (see the bottom photo on the facing page). The idea is to catch the dust at the source before it becomes airborne. Although this fitting position works well, the momentum of the dust coming off the blade still propels some of it past the area the vacuum is able to clean.

Other manufacturers mount the fitting in the lower corner of the cabinet (see the photo below). This isn't as good as a fitting mounted nearer to the guides since few vacuums are powerful enough to pull the dust that distance. This method only

catches the dust that is propelled into the lower corner of the cabinet.

In an effort to trap as much dust as possible, I've set up the bandsaw at the university where I teach with fittings in both positions: under the table and inside the cabinet. This method works the best by far. You must realize, however, that it is impossible to catch all of the dust before it enters the air, so it's still a good idea to wear a dust mask.

A second dust collection port in the lower left-hand corner of the bandsaw cabinet captures dust that gets by the first fitting.

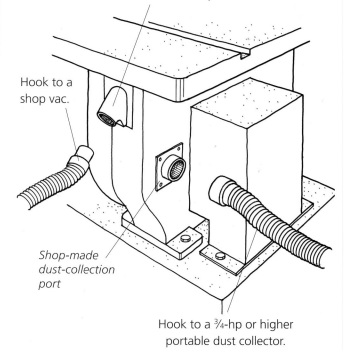

Dust Collection for Resawing

Resawing produces an enormous quantity of very fine wood dust—the kind that is most hazardous to your health. To catch as much dust as possible, use two portable dust collectors hooked up to the bandsaw.

Standard dust-collection port under the table

Hook to a shop vac.

Shop-made dust-collection port

Hook to a ¾-hp or higher portable dust collector.

Tuning Your Bandsaw

Bandsaws are wonderfully versatile machines, but they still need periodic maintenance and adjustment to perform at their peak. And given the flexible nature of the bandsaw blade, you'll be spending a fair bit of time adjusting the guides, since they'll need adjusting at least every time you change the blade, maybe even more. As your saw ages, you'll be dealing with worn tires, bearings, and belts.

Vibration and tracking are common problems, especially for inexpensive consumer bandsaws. In this chapter, I'll discuss how to investigate and repair tracking and vibration problems. But if you're having a difficult time with a bandsaw you've just unpacked, I suggest you return it. These days, because of the fierce competition for your woodworking dollars, it's not difficult to find a well-constructed, smooth-running bandsaw for a reasonable price. On the other hand, it may be well worth your effort to correct flaws on a used machine you picked up at a bargain price. (For more on buying a bandsaw, see chapter 3.)

Many bandsaw problems such as poor tracking, frequent blade breakage, and vibration can be summed up in one word: tires. Smooth-crowned tires are a major key to bandsaw performance, but as tires age they become worn and sometimes develop cracks. Narrow blades can create grooves in your bandsaw's tires, which can make tracking difficult. Pitch, dust, and dirt can build up on tires and cause problems that are similar to those

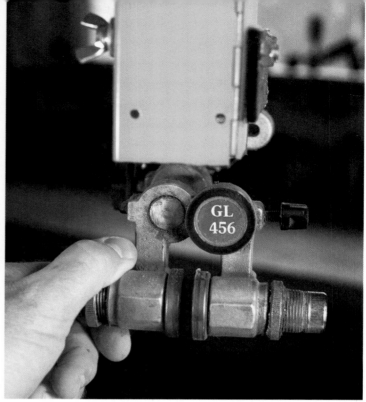

By its very nature, a bandsaw blade is prone to wandering and deflection. For maximum precision, it needs the support of carefully adjusted guides.

When changing blades, open the guides so that they can't interfere with tensioning and tracking the blade.

caused by wear. Fortunately, these and many other bandsaw problems are not difficult to correct.

In this chapter, I'll cover a variety of techniques you can use to keep your bandsaw singing. From tire changes to guide adjustments, it's all here. So read on to discover ways to get peak performance from your bandsaw.

Changing Blades

The different blade widths, tooth forms, and pitches available for your bandsaw are what make it so versatile. As I men-

tioned, if you want to take full advantage of your bandsaw's versatility, you'll have to change blades often. Unfortunately, changing a blade can be a complex job, one that may seem like a chore to avoid. But with some practice, you'll find that it becomes quick and easy. The key is to follow a set of steps in a logical order. For example, you should track the blade before you adjust the guides, otherwise you'll have to adjust them a second time. Because blade tension affects tracking, you'll want to first bring the blade up to proper tension. I've listed the steps in their proper sequence in the sidebar on p. 92.

The Proper Sequence of Bandsaw-Blade Tune-Up

1. Disconnect the power.

2. Release the blade tension. I lower the upper wheel just enough to slip the blade off.

3. Set the guides so they don't interfere with the blade in any way—at the sides or at the back.

4. Install the new blade, first on the upper wheel, then around the lower wheel.

5. Apply just enough tension to take the slack out of the blade.

6. Turn one wheel a few times to move the blade to the center of the tire.

7. Tension the blade with a meter, or if using the saw's gauge, set the tension for the next widest blade.

8. Track the blade.

9. Adjust the upper and lower thrust bearings so they don't quite touch the blade.

10. Set the distance from the upper and lower guides to the blade with a scrap of paper or a dollar bill.

11. Square the table to the blade.

12. Round the back of the blade.

Expensive blades and tension

Bimetal, carbide-tipped, and spring-steel blades can be tensioned significantly tighter than carbon blades. That means they will be more rigid and less likely to deflect and wander in difficult cutting situations, making them an ideal choice for resawing.

When to reduce tension

The less likely a blade is to deflect in a certain kind of cut, the less tension you should put on the blade.

Tensioning Blades

Finding the correct blade tension always seems to be something of a mystery among woodworkers. There are all kinds of methods out there, such as plucking the blade like a guitar string until it produces a clear tone of a specific musical pitch. Although I have no doubt that this method works for a few musically inclined woodworkers, I question its practicality and accuracy for the rest of us. Other theories are even more abstract, such as the notion that you should find the tension that makes your bandsaw "comfortable." To me, this statement seems too vague.

In an effort to avoid adding to the confusion, I'm going to give you some practical ideas on tensioning blades so that you can adjust your saw for accurate cuts. But first I'd like to make some points about bandsaw blades and tension.

Finding the right tension

Bandsaw blades require tension and lots of it to consistently produce straight, uniform cuts, especially in thick or dense stock. Most blade manufacturers recommend 15,000 psi to 20,000 psi for a common carbon-steel blade.

However, bimetal, spring-steel, and carbide-tipped blades are much stronger than carbon-steel blades, so manufacturers recommend a much higher tension: 25,000 psi to 30,000 psi. Why do bandsaw blades need so much tension? For beam strength. The tighter the blade is stretched, the more rigid it becomes and the less tendency it will have to deflect in the cut.

You only need maximum tension for the most demanding cuts, such as sawing dense hardwoods or stock of the maximum thickness that will fit under a saw's guides. In simpler circumstances, you can back off the tension a little.

All blades, regardless of width, require the same amount of tension for maximum beam strength. The variable factor is the amount of pulling force needed. For example, it takes approximately 200 lb. of force pulling on a ¼-in.-wide by 0.025-in.-thick blade to create 25,000 psi of tension. Conversely, a ¾-in.-wide by 0.032-in.-thick blade will require approximately 800 lb. of force to create the same 25,000 psi of tension.

The tension scales on most bandsaws are inaccurate. It's common for scales to indicate a tension far above the actual tension on the blade.

Measuring tension

Bandsaw-blade tension scales are notoriously inaccurate. Tests conducted by consumer woodworking magazines have shown this, and my own tests using six different bandsaws confirmed their results. For my tests, I used a blade tension meter that clamps to the blade and gives an accurate reading on a dial indica-

A meter that clamps onto the blade is the most accurate way to tension a bandsaw blade.

Adjusting tension

You can assume the gauge on your bandsaw reads too low. Set the blade tension at the point indicated for the next wider blade.

tor (see the photo at left). The readings of all the saw tension scales that I tested, including those on the expensive floor-model saws, were lower than that indicated on the meter. Although the scales on the large machines were close to being accurate, the scales on the 14-in. saws were way off. To make matters worse, the springs used in the tension scales on bandsaws weaken with age, further reducing their accuracy.

So how do you know when blade tension is correct? The most accurate way is to check it with a tension meter such as the one I used in my tests. But tension meters are expensive—typically around $300. I know what you're thinking—is there another way? Yes, but none is as accurate as a tension meter. Other tensioning methods will work, but they're a lot like gauging air pressure in a bicycle tire simply by squeezing it.

A good place to begin is to tension the blade until the meter reads proper tension for the next wider blade. For example, if you're tensioning a ⅜-in. blade, I would set the scale to ½ in. This works most of the time, since most sawing operations don't require maximum tension.

Another method is to test the tension by the amount that the blade will deflect sideways. First, I set the upper guides about 6 in. off the table. Then using a moderate amount of pressure from my index finger (obviously with the saw turned off!), I push the blade sideways. I don't want the blade to bow more than ¼ in. (see the photo on the facing page).

Of course, you'll have to develop a feel for how much pressure is moderate.

Although both of these methods work, they are imprecise. But as I stated earlier, in most situations maximum blade tension isn't necessary. I always test the blade tension with a trial piece before making cuts in an actual workpiece. If the blade wanders in the cut (assuming other factors such as blade sharpness and guide setting are correct), I'll gradually increase the blade tension.

Blade tensioning for resawing

Resawing thick, hard stock places the most demands on the blade. If the blade tension is inadequate, the blade will bow and the stock may be spoiled (see the drawing on p. 96).

I remember a situation some years ago when I attempted to resaw a wide board. It was a plank of deep red cherry—highly figured with truly awesome curly grain. I wanted to make book-matched panels for a door in a cupboard. Since I was in a hurry, I neglected the necessary precautions such as selecting a blade with the right pitch and tensioning it properly. The blade bowed badly during cutting, making one of the planks terribly thin at the end. The stock was thicker than necessary, so I was lucky enough just to squeeze out the thickness I needed from the resawn plank. But I learned my lesson: A blade needs beam strength for resawing.

Beam strength, the blade's ability to resist deflection, is achieved by combining several factors, including correct blade

If you don't have a tension meter, you can roughly tension the blade by eye. Raise the guides about 6 in. off the table and push the blade. The blade should deflect no more than ¼ in.

When the blade vibrates

The array of running gear on a bandsaw (tires, wheels, pulleys, belts, blade, etc.) can set up harmonic vibrations even when everything else is right. If that happens to you, try changing the blade tension slightly, either more or less, just enough to change the harmonic.

Inadequate Blade Tension Causes Bowing

If the blade is not tight enough, it can bow in the cut, often ruining the stock.

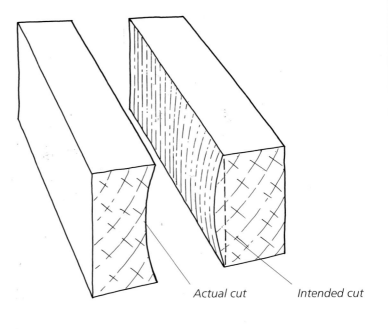

Actual cut   *Intended cut*

Don't fully compress the spring

I don't recommend completely compressing the tension spring. You might get more tension, but the spring is there to absorb minor vibration or slight bounces during cutting. The spring helps prevent the blade from breaking.

pitch, blade width, and precise guide settings. But a key factor in achieving beam strength is applying the maximum blade tension that the blade manufacturer recommends.

Some woodworkers may question whether maximum blade tension will in any way damage the saw. Based on years of experience with my 14-in. Delta bandsaw, the answer is no. But I should make it clear that I recommend using maximum blade tension only for occasional, brief periods of resawing. Otherwise, I keep the tension low for everyday sawing. I release the tension when I know I won't be using the saw for a while.

If you've purchased a bandsaw with a wheel diameter of 18 in. or more, then you're most likely planning to do serious resawing from time to time. In that case, I suggest that you also spend the money on a tension meter. Large bandsaws have frames that are capable of overtensioning a blade, which causes it to break. A tension meter is the most accurate way of setting the blade tension.

If you own one of the many consumer bandsaws with a wheel diameter of 14 in. or less, then I would use a blade no wider than ½ in. for resawing and tension it until the tension spring is nearly compressed (see the photo at right).

Tracking

Tracking a blade involves tilting the upper wheel, which causes the blade to ride in the center of the tire. If the wheels of the saw are in alignment and the tires are crowned, the blade should track entirely on its own without having to tilt the upper wheel. Then why have the tracking adjustment? It compensates for slight wheel misalignments that naturally occur when you tension a blade (see the drawing on p. 98). When the blade is tensioned, it places several hundred pounds of force on the wheels, a force that is easily enough to cause wheel misalignment on even the largest industrial bandsaws.

If you have a new bandsaw that won't track a blade, I recommend that you

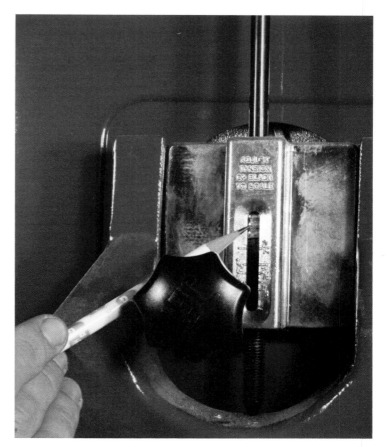

On a small consumer-grade bandsaw, I tension a ½-in. blade for resawing by almost completely compressing the tension spring.

If your bandsaw won't track

Severe misalignment is rare in bandsaws. If even careful adjustment won't keep your blades on track, it may mean that the wheels are warped or the frame is bent.

Tracking a Blade

Most bandsaws don't need a tracking adjustment until the blade is tensioned at or near the maximum. That is when the upper wheel may become misaligned so that the blade won't track on the center of the tires. You can easily correct the misalignment by carefully turning the tracking knob until the blade settles on the center of the tires.

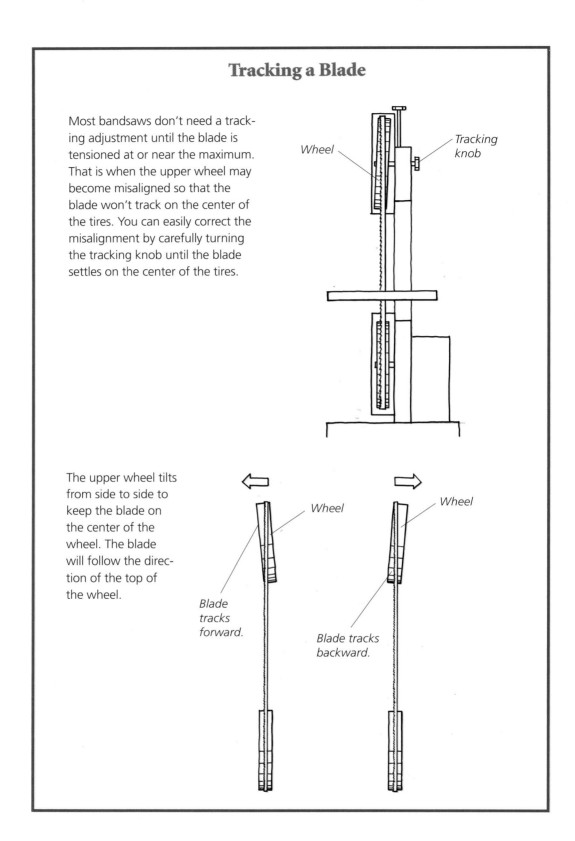

Wheel

Tracking knob

The upper wheel tilts from side to side to keep the blade on the center of the wheel. The blade will follow the direction of the top of the wheel.

Wheel

Wheel

Blade tracks forward.

Blade tracks backward.

return the saw. If your bandsaw won't tension and track a blade, then you need a better saw.

To track a blade once it's tensioned, spin the top wheel with one hand while slowly turning the tracking knob with the other (see the photo at right). The blade will travel in the direction of the tilt. All new bandsaws have crowned tires, and the blade should track at the crown's center point. The crown on large bandsaws is very slight to give wide blades better support.

Once the blade is consistently tracking, lock the setting with the lock nut on the tracking screw, then close the covers and momentarily turn on the power for a final check of the tracking.

Adjusting the Guides

For accurate cutting, the blade needs to be fully supported at the back and at the sides both above and below the table. The goal is to set the guides so that they aren't in contact with the blade until the blade starts to wander. When the saw isn't running, set the guides right next to the blade but not touching it.

The upper and lower thrust wheels support the back of the blade to prevent feed pressure from pushing it off the saw's wheels. Set them just slightly behind the blade. They should not spin until the stock is fed into the blade.

The side blocks or bearings prevent the blade from twisting or bowing sideways. Like the thrust wheel, the side supports should contact the blade only when there

Tracking the blade is a two-handed job. Spin the upper wheel while adjusting the tracking knob until the blade rides on the center of the tire.

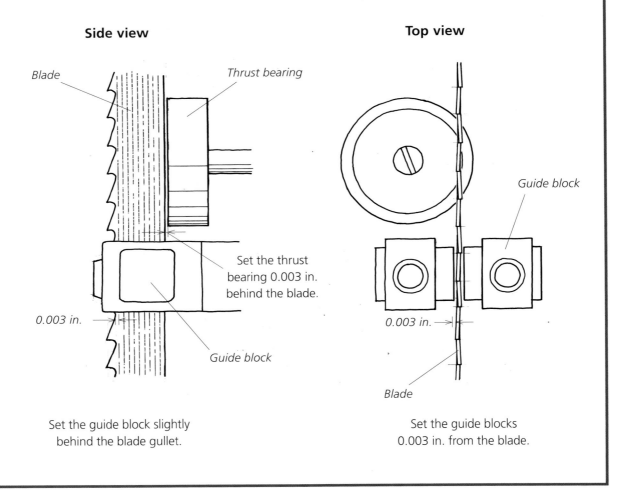

Adjusting the Thrust Bearings and Guides

The thrust bearings and guides surround the blade and keep it from bowing, twisting, or wandering in a cut. Adjust them so they are not touching the blade when the saw is idle but will come in contact with the blade the instant you start sawing.

Side view

Blade

Thrust bearing

Set the thrust bearing 0.003 in. behind the blade.

0.003 in.

Guide block

Set the guide block slightly behind the blade gullet.

Top view

Guide block

0.003 in.

Blade

Set the guide blocks 0.003 in. from the blade.

is pressure from cutting. But if the side supports are set too far from the blade, the blade will wander, making it difficult to saw accurately.

To prevent damaging the teeth of the blade, set the guides. First, set the guides behind the gullets (see the drawing

above). Then slip a piece of paper or a dollar bill between each guide and the blade, and bring the guide toward the blade until it barely grips the paper (see the bottom photo on p. 102). Lock the guide in place before removing the paper.

Rounding the Back of the Blade

A blade with back corners that have been slightly rounded cuts smoother, tighter curves and increases the life of your thrust bearings (see the drawing below). You can buy a special stone for honing the backs of your bandsaw blades at a woodworking specialty store. To use it, simply hold the stone on the tabletop with the blade running and bevel the back corners. Then slowly rotate the stone around the back of the blade, rounding the corners.

When the back corners of the blade have been rounded, the blades slide around tight curves more readily.

Blade not rounded

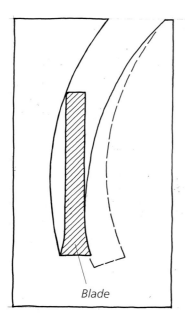

Blade

The curve is not as tight. There is a twisting force on the blade.

Blade rounded

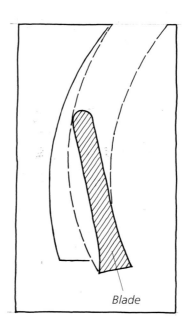

Blade

The corner of the blade does not interfere. The rounded back slides along the kerf.

Mounting a ¹⁄₁₆-in.-wide Blade

A narrow ¹⁄₁₆-in. scrolling blade has very little blade body, which makes it impossible to run with the block or bearing guides. When the blocks are set far enough back from the gullet to protect the teeth, they don't adequately support the blade.

If you have block guides, you can run a blade this narrow by replacing the steel blocks with "Cool Blocks." Cool Blocks are made from a fibrous material that is impregnated with a dry lubricant. It is soft enough to surround the blade without damage to the teeth. Instead of Cool Blocks, you can also use hardwood. I make the guide blocks for my bandsaw from scraps of maple or cherry.

Before I mount the blocks into the guide frame, I cut a very small notch into one of the blocks for the blade to ride in. Then when I mount the blocks in the guide frame, I pinch them together so that they completely surround the tiny blade.

To guide a ¹⁄₁₆-in.-wide blade, replace the steel guide blocks with shopmade wooden blocks. Cut a notch in one block, and support the blade by completely surrounding it.

You don't need a feeler gauge to set guides. Just adjust the guides so they don't quite grip a scrap of paper set between them and the blade.

Vibration Problems

Vibration is probably the most common bandsaw problem and certainly the most annoying. Because the bandsaw has so many moving parts, any number of things, such as the tires, wheels, motor, pulleys, or belt, may cause the vibration. Even a flimsy sheet-metal stand can contribute to the problem. The good news is that these problems are easy to trace, and most are easy to repair.

Tires

Bandsaw tires cushion the blade and provide traction to power the blade. With the exception of some older bandsaws, most bandsaws have crowned tires in which the middle of the tire is higher and slopes

Most new bandsaws have crowned wheels so it's unnecessary to crown the tire after installation. This wheel also has a channel to hold the tire in place.

Crowned Tires Keep the Blade on Track

The blade naturally rides on the slightly higher middle of a crowned wheel or tire.

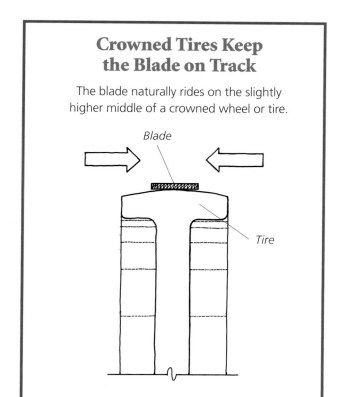

Blade

Tire

Keep the tires clean

Clean tires make for consistent tracking and smooth performance. Pitch, dirt, and fine dust on the tires can cause the blade to bounce, wander, and vibrate. You can remove this buildup by using mineral spirits and a stiff brush. To help keep the tires clean, mount a stiff brush on the saw frame to sweep the tires as the saw is running. A dust collector also helps.

slightly toward the edges. Crowned tires make it easier to keep blades properly tracking since they naturally tend to ride on the highest point of the crown (see the drawing above). The tires on large bandsaws have relatively less crown for better support of wider blades.

Age and use cause grooves and unevenness in bandsaw tires and eventually the loss of the crown. When this occurs, you'll experience blade vibration and bouncing and difficulty in keeping the blade tracking. Fortunately, changing tires is not difficult, especially on small bandsaws.

The process involves just three steps: removing the old tire, stretching the new tire around the rim, and gluing it in place. To simplify the process further, many new bandsaws have a channel milled into the rim of the wheel, which makes it easier to center the tire. Better yet, the surface of the channel is crowned and the tire conforms to it, making it unnecessary to crown the tire (see the photo above).

Some bandsaws have tires that simply snap into a groove that is milled into the rim of the wheel (see the drawing on p. 104). Without question, this is the easiest type to change, but it does require that you purchase a special tire from the manufacturer of your saw.

Recrowning worn tires If you're having difficulty tracking a blade (especially a narrow one), the first thing you should try is recrowning the tires. The difference

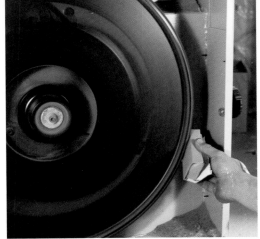

If the tires have worn slightly, you can easily reshape the crown with a sanding block while the wheels are turning (but not with the blade installed).

The Easiest Bandsaw Tire to Change

This specially designed tire simply snaps into a groove milled into the wheel. It doesn't need to be glued or crowned.

Tire

Snap-in groove

Wheel

Spinning the upper wheel

For recrowning, you can run the lower wheel by the motor. For the upper wheel, have a helper spin the top by holding a sanding drum chucked into a portable drill against the tire.

between the crown and the sides of the tire should be about $\frac{1}{32}$ in. If that's not enough to keep the blade on track, try $\frac{1}{16}$ in. The amount of crown required to keep the blade tracking is very small.

If the tires are thick enough, you can recrown the surface with sandpaper. I wrap the sandpaper around a wood block and gradually reshape the tire while the wheel is spinning (see the photo above). Don't attempt this with a blade on the saw! You can run the lower wheel with the motor and have a friend spin the top wheel with a sanding drum chucked into a portable drill. This method works well with tires that have slight wear, such as the loss of the crown. But if your saw's tires have severe wear or age cracks, then it's time to replace them.

Replacing tires I've done repair work on several bandsaws, each of which used a different arrangement for fastening the wheels to the shaft. If you're in doubt about the best way to remove the wheels, review the drawing in the manual for the saw (if it's available).

Once the wheel is off, lay it on a workbench, then cut the tire with a utility knife and start prying it off. If the tire isn't glued in place, it may simply fall off the rim, but most tires are glued on. If the tires were not glued on, I would still recommend gluing on the new ones.

I've found that the level of difficulty in removing a tire depends upon its age and condition. Cracked tires come off in pieces, but typically a tire peels off the rim in a long strip. You'll have to remove all traces of old tire and glue so that the new tire can seat evenly.

With all remnants of old tire and glue gone, stretch the new tires over the wheels. To ensure a tight fit, new tires are approximately 20% smaller than the wheels.

I always glue the tires in place because I've seen tires slip when resawing wide boards. When this happens, the saw will shudder violently for a brief moment. It's very annoying and nerve-racking, and it doesn't do the bandsaw a heck of a lot of good, either.

This happened recently with a friend's 14-in. bandsaw. At first we thought the drive belt was slipping, but it checked out as tight enough. Then I suspected the tires. To test the hypothesis, we marked each tire and rim with a pen before making another test cut with a slow, steady feed (see the drawing at right). The saw shuddered and squealed as before. When we opened the cover and examined the marks, they were misaligned by ½ in. on both wheels. Gluing on the tires solved the problem.

Gluing the tires in place is much easier after the tires are stretched over the wheels. Otherwise, the procedure becomes a sticky mess. I'll get back to gluing, but first I'll discuss getting the tire on the rim. Think of the tire as an oversized rubber band that you'll have to stretch around the wheel. Stretching the tires around wheels 14-in. and smaller is easy, but you'll most likely need help for anything larger. Still, the process isn't difficult—it's just more than two hands can manage.

To begin, position the wheel vertically on the floor over the tire. Next, you and a friend should each stretch the tire around the wheel in opposite directions. As the tire is stretched it will have a tendency to slip off the rim, so you should each hold the tire in position with one hand while

Removing tire adhesive

To soften tire adhesive, I use lacquer thinner. A small squeeze bottle makes it easy to get the thinner around the edge of the tire. A flat, sharp stick of wood works well as a scraper, and it doesn't damage aluminum wheels. Remember to have plenty of ventilation when using lacquer thinner. Besides being flammable, the fumes are harmful to breathe.

Check for Slipping Tires

If you suspect the tires on your bandsaw are slipping, mark the tire and rim with a felt-tip pen. Saw a test board with a slow, steady feed, then check the marks. If they're no longer lined up, the tires are slipping. Solve the problem by gluing the tires down.

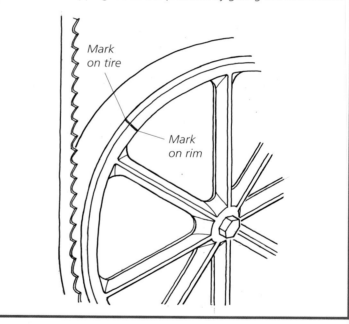

Mark on tire

Mark on rim

pulling, stretching, and positioning the tire with the other. The process takes less than two minutes.

The next step is to apply the glue. I use 3M weather-stripping adhesive. To get under the tire, insert a short length of pipe or wooden dowel between the tire

A dowel raises the tire off the rim so you can apply the glue underneath it with a small brush.

and rim. This raises the tire just enough so you can apply glue to the surfaces with a brush (see the photo above). By rolling the dowel around the rim, it's possible to apply glue to the entire perimeter. Allow the glue to set overnight.

If your wheels aren't crowned, you'll have to crown the tires once the glue is dry. Use a sanding block and sandpaper as described on pp. 103-104 for recrowning worn tires.

I've read that you should trim the tires after mounting to make them concentric, but I've never seen tire unevenness to be a problem. Not long ago, I helped a friend install tires on his old 20-in. bandsaw. Afterwards we checked tire runout with a dial indicator and found that it was within 0.010 in., which is close enough for saw smoothness and closer than I could get with any shop-built trimming jig.

Wheels

Wheels can contribute to vibration in one of several ways. The wheels could have bearing problems, they may not be round, or they could be unbalanced.

Bearings When examining wheels, the first thing to check is the bearings. Remove the blade and drive belt so they don't interfere with your inspection, then spin each wheel slowly and listen for clicking or grinding. Good bearings are smooth and quiet.

If you suspect that a bearing is worn, you can have it replaced at a local machine shop or you can do it yourself. You can remove the old bearing by resting the wheel on a workbench and knocking the bearing out with a hammer and a wood block. Then press the new bearing in place by laying a block of wood over the bearing and applying pressure with a clamp.

Roundness Old bandsaw wheels can get distorted from years of blade tension; if a new wheel is out-of-round it's because of sloppy machining. You can check for wheel roundness with a dial indicator that attaches to the frame of the saw. For an accurate reading, position the indicator tip at the edge of the machined rim of the wheel. The wheel probably won't be perfect, but if it is off by more than 0.025 in., it's enough to cause vibration.

A machine shop can true the wheel, but unless you have a large industrial bandsaw, the cost of the machining may exceed the value of the saw. Alternatively, you may be able to get a new wheel from the manufacturer.

Wheel balance To check wheel balance, spin the wheel (with the blade and drive belt removed) and allow it to coast to a stop. Mark the lowest point of the wheel

Troubleshooting Bandsaw Problems

Problem	Diagnosis	
The blade hops or bounces while running.	• Chunks of the tire are missing. • Chunks of the drive belt are missing.	• The pulleys are bent. • The blade has a sharp bend or kink.
The blade moves in and out while running.	• The blade weld is misaligned.	• There is sawdust and pitch buildup on the tires.
The blade bows during resawing and spoils the workpiece.	• The blade pitch is too fine. • There is buildup of pitch in the blade gullets.	• The blade is dull. • The feed rate is too fast.
The blade is difficult to track.	• Excess tension has distorted the frame and caused severe wheel misalignment. Decrease the blade tension.	• The tires are worn or dirty.
The sawblade wanders in the cut.	• The feed rate is too fast.	• The guides are not set closely enough.
The blade breaks prematurely.	• The weld is poor. • There is excessive tension. *Note*: This is really only a problem with large saws (20 in. and above) or very narrow blades (1/16 in. and 1/8 in.).	• The wheel is too small for the blade thickness. • A turn in the stock is too tight for the blade width.
There is a ticking sound.	• There is excess flash at the weld. • There is a stress crack in the blade.	• There is a kink in the blade.
The blade dulls quickly.	• The blade was overheated (too fine a pitch).	• Incorrectly set guides pushed the set from the teeth.
There is excessive vibration.	• The tires are dirty. • The wheels are out of balance or out of round. • A cheap motor is out of balance, has a flimsy motor mount, or has loose mounting fasteners.	• The tires are extremely worn. • Cheap pulleys are out of round. • The pulleys are loose or misaligned. • The drive belt is worn. • The sheet-metal stand is flimsy.
The blade shudders when resawing.	• The drive belt slipped momentarily.	• The tires slipped momentarily.

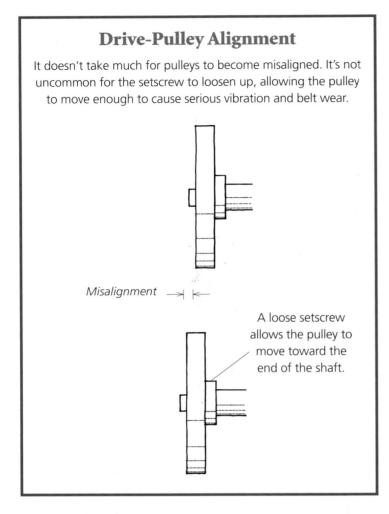

Drive-Pulley Alignment

It doesn't take much for pulleys to become misaligned. It's not uncommon for the setscrew to loosen up, allowing the pulley to move enough to cause serious vibration and belt wear.

Misalignment →| |←

A loose setscrew allows the pulley to move toward the end of the shaft.

Many bandsaw manufacturers dynamically balance the wheels of their saws. One I spoke to said that his company balances the wheels to within 0.3 grams at 700 rpm. I don't doubt this claim; the saw that I tried was very smooth indeed.

Motors

Good motors are balanced to provide a smooth, vibration-free power source. In preparation for this book, I tested several well-known brands of bandsaws. One 14-in. saw ran incredibly smoothly. When I mentioned this to the manufacturer, I learned the details about how the company achieves such smooth performance in a competitively priced saw. One of the keys was the motor, which they balanced to 0.3 grams at 1,700 rpm. I was surprised to find such attention to quality on a consumer bandsaw.

To test the motor on your saw for excessive vibration, run the motor without the drive belt and pulley. If the motor doesn't run smoothly, check the motor mount for loose fasteners. If it's well mounted, look for a replacement motor. I suggest buying a name-brand American-made motor. It's a good opportunity to increase the horsepower.

Drive pulleys

Recently, one of the bandsaws at the university where I teach began vibrating and making a terrible racket. Since this was out of character for the machine, I immediately suspected a loose pulley. On opening the stand, I discovered that the wheel pulley was indeed loose and had vibrated

and spin it several more times, each time marking the lowest point. If the wheel is out of balance, the same point will keep ending up at the bottom.

You can lighten that area of the rim by drilling shallow ⅜-in. holes in it, but be careful to avoid removing too much metal. Spin the wheel several times more. When it no longer stops at the same point, it is as close to balanced as you can get using this method.

out to the end of the wheel shaft, which caused severe drive-belt misalignment.

Vibration problems aren't typically as simple as this one, but pulleys can sometimes be the problem. When checking pulleys, look for the obvious first: looseness or misalignment (see the drawing on the facing page). Otherwise, the problem might be the pulleys themselves.

Inexpensive bandsaws generally have die-cast pulleys that are not perfectly round or the shaft hole isn't centered. You can spot pulleys that have been machined round to improve balance by the concentric rings in the surface that were created during the turning process. If your pulleys don't have those rings, replacing the pulleys will go a long way to reduce your saw's vibration.

Drive belts

I stepped into my shop one day and turned on my old Rockwell Unisaw to make a cut. The vibration was incredible, especially since this saw is normally very smooth. I pulled the power cord from the wall, crawled under the saw, and found that one of the belts in the triple-belt drive system had big chunks missing. The same thing will happen when a bandsaw's belts are worn out.

But it doesn't take a worn belt to create vibration problems. A poor-quality belt may have lumps or inconsistencies in the V-profile, which rides in the groove around the rim of the pulley.

Check the table for square against a tensioned blade.

Tables

Most bandsaws have a tilting table with an adjustable stop to accurately reset the table to 90°. To adjust the table, mount a ½-in.-wide blade, tension it, and back off the guides so that they don't interfere with the table setting. Place a reliable square on the table, and turn the stop-adjusting screw until the blade of the square is parallel to the sawblade.

> ### Pay attention to drive belts
>
> Drive belts are much more sophisticated than they look. An inexpensive belt is no bargain. You can buy high-quality V-belts at auto supply stores. Many woodworking specialty suppliers have link belts, which are also great for minimizing vibration.

Thrust-Bearing Problems

The best thrust bearing is a hardened steel disk pressed over a sealed bearing. Unfortunately, this design is used only on more expensive saws. The thrust bearing

The thrust bearing on the left is new; the one on the right is severely worn and needs replacing.

gives more problems than the upper bearing because pitch and dust from the downward movement of the blade continually bombard it. As the pitch builds up, the bearing doesn't spin freely, so the blade wears grooves in the face of the bearing. This in turn causes the back of the blade to heat excessively, which leads to fatigue and breakage.

This whole scenario is easy to avoid by removing the lower thrust bearing occasionally and cleaning off the pitch. Even so, the lower bearing needs to be replaced more often than the upper one. This is an inexpensive part that you can find locally at a bearing or motor repair shop. I usually keep a couple of replacement bearings on hand.

Guide-Block Maintenance

If your saw has steel guide blocks, you'll need to true them up occasionally with a file or grinder. Over a long period of use, the blocks become worn, and steps form in the face of the block, which limit the effectiveness of the guide (see the drawing at left). It takes only a few minutes to reface the block.

I don't recommend replacing the steel blocks in your saw with plastic blocks. Compared to steel blocks, plastic blocks wear out very quickly and they offer no real advantages. Inexpensive carbon-steel blades may become overheated at the tooth tip during resawing, but plastic blocks won't eliminate the overheating, just as steel blocks are not the cause of it.

Step-Worn Guide Blocks

The bearing surfaces of guide blocks (even steel ones) become worn. Narrow blades are the worst because they wear a step into the block, which greatly decreases the block's effectiveness. All guide blocks need their bearing surfaces trued up from time to time.

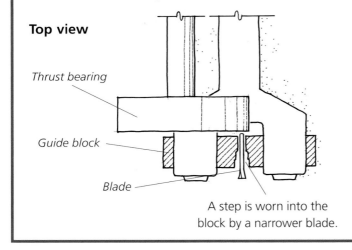

Top view

Thrust bearing

Guide block

Blade

A step is worn into the block by a narrower blade.

Keep guide blocks square

Whether you use sandpaper, a file, or a grinder to true up the face of your guide blocks, check your progress frequently with a small square.

on most consumer bandsaws is simply a bearing mounted on a shaft, and the blade is supported on the edge of the bearing face.

The thrust bearing on the lower guide typically

Basic Bandsaw Techniques

Perhaps no other woodworking machine has greater appeal than the bandsaw. No matter what your area of woodworking interest, the bandsaw has a use. If you enjoy carving, for example, the bandsaw is indispensable for roughing out blanks. If you're a woodturner, the bandsaw is a great companion to the lathe for sizing stock for a bowl. For the furniture maker, the bandsaw is an essential tool for everything from ripping rough stock to creating curves. And because the bandsaw is relatively safe when compared to other woodworking machines, you'll find that using it can be an enjoyable experience as well.

If you're new to the bandsaw, you'll also find that the machine is easy to learn how to use. After just a few minutes of practice, most people are up to guiding the stock through the turns to make a delicate table apron or even a sculpted leg for a chair. But don't feel that the bandsaw is limited to curves. Although the bandsaw is *the* tool for creating curves, it is sometimes the safest and easiest way to rip wide boards into narrower widths.

In this chapter, I'll cover the basics of using the bandsaw for cutting curves and ripping, along with some information on removing tool marks. One word of advice before you begin: Review the safety guidelines in chapter 5 and always make safety a priority when using this versatile tool.

How to Cut Curves

No other woodworking machine can cut curves as quickly, easily, and accurately as the bandsaw. When compared to other machines designed for cutting curves,

No other woodworking machine cuts curves as quickly and precisely as the bandsaw.

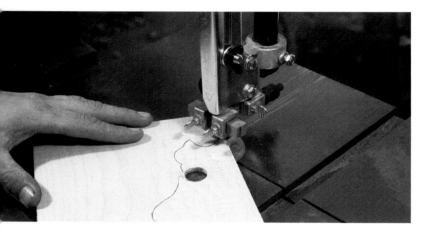

Equipped with a narrow blade, the bandsaw excels at cutting scrolls. Note the drilled hole used to make the tightest curve.

such as the scrollsaw or the jigsaw, the bandsaw has greater power and cutting depth. In many situations, the bandsaw cuts more smoothly, too. That's because a bandsaw blade continuously cuts downward but a scrollsaw blade or jigsaw blade has an erratic reciprocating movement. When equipped with the right blade, a bandsaw is much more versatile, too, since it can cut broad, shallow curves or tight, ornate scrolls.

Curved Moldings

Curved moldings, such as those in the hood of this clock, can create a dramatic effect for your work.

Curved moldings are found extensively on both furniture and architectural woodworking from the 18th and 19th centuries. Curved moldings are typically either part of a true circle, such as a molding strip on the hood of a clock, or a cyma curve, such as those seen on the pediments of casework. The curved moldings on pediments are called gooseneck moldings. They often terminate in a round carving called a rosette.

Whether or not you enjoy reproducing colonial American furniture, you may still find the bandsaw techniques for making curved moldings useful for other projects and furniture styles.

Making curved moldings involves more than just bandsawing a curve into the stock. After sawing the contour, the molding profile must be shaped on the stock with a shaper or a router. The curved stock can't be guided by a straight fence, as is normally the case when shaping moldings. Instead, the workpiece is guided by either a curved fence or a rub bearing, which is mounted on the router or shaper. Let's look at the process so that you'll have a better understanding of the steps involved in making curved moldings.

Begin by sawing only the reference surface. Rather than bandsawing both the inside and outside radii of a curved molding, bandsaw only the surface that will be molded (see the top drawing at right). This makes shaping or routing safer and more precise because the extra mass reduces vibration and provides you with a better grip and control of the stock.

Avoid short grain. Areas of short grain are weak and may break during shaping or when applying the molding. As a general rule, curved molding sections shouldn't exceed a quarter turn (90°) in order to avoid short grain. For example, use two 90° sections to produce a 180° turn (see the bottom drawing at right).

Use plywood templates. Whenever I make curved moldings, I lay out and bandsaw the curve onto ½-in. plywood for use as a template. Once made, the template serves three purposes. First, it becomes a pattern for tracing the curve to the workpiece. Second, you can quickly remove the bandsaw marks from the workpiece by securing the workpiece to the template and flush-trimming with a router. Third, the template serves as a bearing guide when shaping the molding profile.

Bandsaw the opposite radius once the shaping is complete. Take your time. The most common mistake is to saw too fast. By taking your time, you can achieve much more accurate results and avoid the tedious job of smoothing away errors with a file.

Preparing Stock for Making Curved Moldings

Molding the profile into a piece of curved stock will be much safer and more accurate if you have a substantial workpiece to run through a router or a shaper.

Extra stock provides a safe and secure grip while shaping or routing.

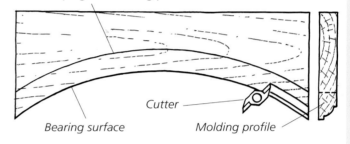

Don't bandsaw this curve until after shaping the molding profile.

Cutter

Bearing surface

Molding profile

Avoid Short Grain in Curves

When bandsawing segments of a true circle, avoid short, weak grain by using a separate plank for each quarter of the circle.

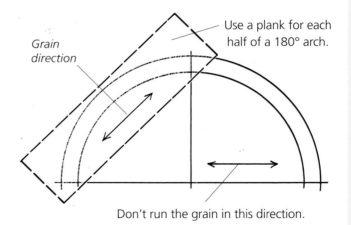

Grain direction

Use a plank for each half of a 180° arch.

Don't run the grain in this direction.

A pattern is the key to laying out great curves. I make mine out of plywood and mark all pertinent information on it for the next time I use it.

Changing the Scale of a Pattern

Although I usually draw my own designs for patterns, I sometimes use an existing design from a book or magazine. When drawn for publication, most patterns must be scaled down to fit the page. To make the design easy to enlarge, it's presented on a grid so that you can reference from the squares of the grid. To enlarge the design from the grid, you'll first have to draw a new grid with squares measuring the dimension given. Then you can re-create the curves of the design by plotting points on the grid and connecting them. This method works well, but it can be slow and tedious.

Instead, I prefer to use a photocopier. Most photocopiers can not only enlarge but can also do so in 1% increments. To use this method, I measure the squares on the copy and enlarge them until they equal the size indicated on the original drawing. Although most photocopiers will create a slight amount of distortion when enlarging, it is easy to correct when making the plywood pattern. If your pattern is large, you may want to go to a copy shop that caters to architects and engineers, where they typically have photocopy machines large enough to handle blueprints.

Once I have my enlarged drawing, I glue the paper to the plywood with rubber cement, which doesn't wrinkle paper as white or yellow glues will, and cut the pattern on a bandsaw.

Laying out curves

A good pattern is the key to bandsawing a great-looking curve. I never sketch a curve or design directly on the stock and begin sawing. Instead, I draw my design on thin plywood and cut it out for use as a pattern. This method has three distinct advantages. First, it enables me to get a better concept of the design once it is cut out on plywood. If I'm not satisfied with the outline of the curve, its scale, or its proportion, I can easily and inexpensively modify the pattern or make a new one. Second, it makes it easy to duplicate the curve, as when making four identical legs for a table or chair. Third, if the design is a complex series of twists and turns, I can get a more accurate result if I simply make a pattern for one-half of the design. By flipping the pattern over when tracing it on the workpiece, I get a perfectly symmetrical layout.

I sketch the curve on the plywood, checking, erasing, and redrawing until I'm satisfied with the design. Next, I carefully bandsaw the pattern and smooth the edges with a spindle sander and various sizes of files until they are free of lumps

The best pattern material

I like to use ¼-in. birch plywood for patterns because it is stiff and its light color enables me to see my sketch. Also, the edges of plywood won't curl or become frayed as paper or cardboard will.

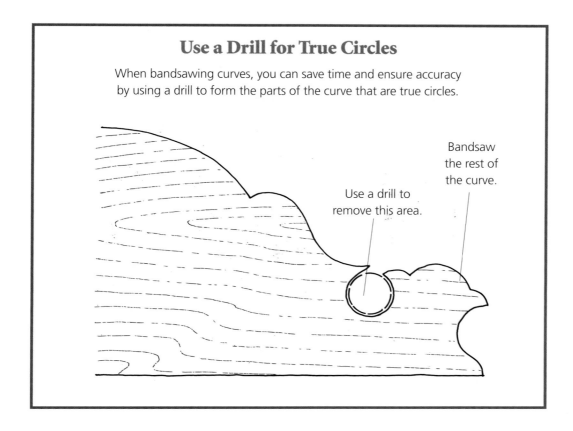

Use a Drill for True Circles

When bandsawing curves, you can save time and ensure accuracy by using a drill to form the parts of the curve that are true circles.

Use a drill to remove this area.

Bandsaw the rest of the curve.

and dead, or flat, spots. Once I'm satisfied with the pattern, I trace it onto the stock.

My plywood patterns are valuable data storage centers, too, because I write construction notes for future reference on the face of my patterns. Information such as the location of a mortise in the leg, the finished diameter of the ankle after sawing and shaping, and the required stock dimensions will be invaluable data when I want to build the same piece of furniture sometime in the future.

When laying out a complex pattern, keep your eye out for contours that are portions of true circles (see the drawing above). One way you can save a lot of

Drill first, then saw

A technique you can use to save time when sawing contours is to use a drill to contour any parts of true circles. It's faster and more precise than sawing. Always do the drilling first, then the bandsawing. Otherwise, the drill bit may wander off center and miscut the stock. You can stack several pieces and drill them together to save time.

time when sawing contours is to drill any true circles. Besides being faster than bandsawing, it's also more precise because it yields a true circle or part of a circle.

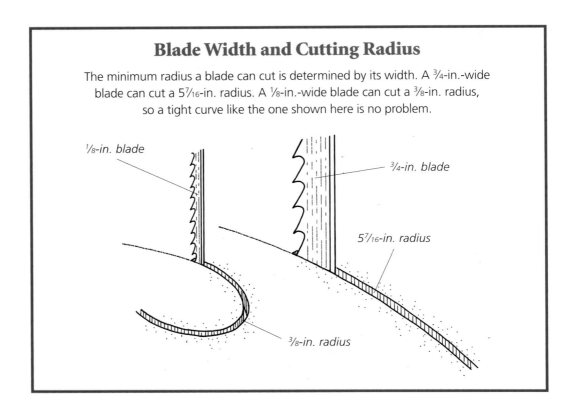

Blade Width and Cutting Radius

The minimum radius a blade can cut is determined by its width. A ¾-in.-wide blade can cut a 5⁷⁄₁₆-in. radius. A ⅛-in.-wide blade can cut a ⅜-in. radius, so a tight curve like the one shown here is no problem.

⅛-in. blade

¾-in. blade

5⁷⁄₁₆-in. radius

⅜-in. radius

Choosing a blade for cutting curves

With so many combinations of material, width, pitch, and tooth form available, choosing a blade for cutting curves can seem like a formidable task. The right blade for sawing a particular curve takes into account a number of factors, such as the radius of the curve, the size of the bandsaw, and the thickness of the stock. Let's look at some of the things you need to consider when selecting a blade for cutting curves.

Blade width The minimum radius that you can cut on your bandsaw is determined by the blade width (see the drawing above). As you follow the layout line

while cutting, you must rotate the workpiece around the blade. The narrower the blade, the tighter the radius you can cut. If you attempt to cut a curve that is too tight for the width of the blade, the blade may break or pull off the wheels.

So why not just mount a narrow blade and cut all curves with that? The difficulty is that cuts tend to wander more with narrow blades. When you're scrolling around tight curves, it's not a problem, but if you're cutting the broad curves of a chair rocker, your line will be distinctly wavy unless you are very skilled.

When you're first learning to cut curves, you'll most likely find a blade-radius chart to be helpful. It will show you the minimum radius that you can cut

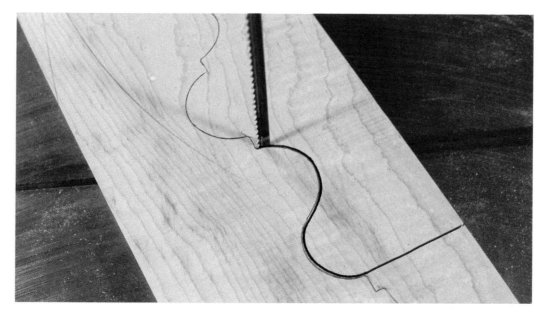

Plan your cutting sequence to avoid trapping the blade.

with the various blade widths available. There's a chart for your reference on p. 74.

Tooth form More than any other factor, tooth form determines how a blade will cut. When smoothness is a concern, the best choice is a regular-tooth blade. Because of their 0° rake angles, regular-tooth blades cut with a smooth, scraping action. In addition, they have the greatest number of teeth, which also contributes to their smooth cutting.

When the curve to be cut is broad and the stock is thick, I'll reach for a hook-tooth blade. Hook blades have positive rake angles and little feed resistance, features that make them well suited for sawing curves in thick stock. I cut all curves with either a hook-tooth blade or a regular-tooth blade.

Pitch It's best to have 6 to 12 teeth in contact with the stock at any given time. A blade on the finer end of that range will produce a smooth surface on the stock. If you go too fine and have more than 12 teeth in the stock, the gullets may become packed with sawdust and the teeth will overheat. The stock may burn, and the heat will severely shorten the life of the blade.

Cutting sequence

An important consideration when sawing contours is the sequence of the cuts. Many designs are made with a series of interconnected cuts. If you don't plan the cutting sequence, you may find yourself trapped in a corner. If you back the sawblade out of the kerf to get out of the corner, you risk pulling the blade off the wheels or breaking it.

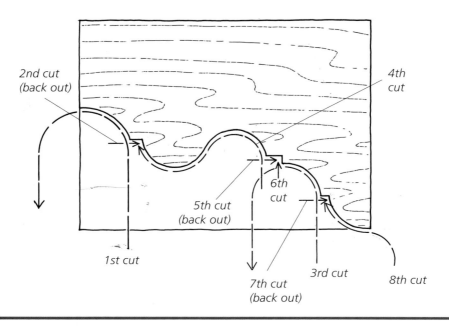

Plan the Sequence of Cuts

When cutting a complex pattern, take the time to plan your cutting sequence to avoid trapping the blade or backing out of long curves.

2nd cut
(back out)

4th
cut

6th
cut

5th cut
(back out)

1st cut

7th cut
(back out)

3rd cut

8th cut

If you get stuck

If you must back out of a curve, stop the saw and use a block of wood to push the blade back against the thrust bearing while you ease the workpiece around the curve and away from the blade.

To avoid such scenarios, I first make a quick analysis of the cutting sequence. The cuts I make first are those that allow me to turn and exit the stock without being trapped in an inside corner (see the drawing above). When two lines of the layout connect at an inside corner, I make the shortest, straightest cut first, then I back out and make the second cut. When backing out of a short, straight kerf, there is little risk of pulling the blade off of the wheels. When two curved cuts interconnect, I first make a straight relief cut to the inside corner. This lets me avoid backing out of a curve.

If necessary, you can relieve stress on the blade when negotiating a turn that is too tight by making a series of relief kerfs down to the line. Then you can clean up the curve by sawing a series of short straight lines around the curve as close to the line as possible (see the drawing on the facing page). This idea has been promoted to avoid changing blades,

When the Blade Is Too Wide for a Curve

If you can't change blades and you don't mind a distinctly choppy appearance,
you can use relief cuts to make a series of straight lines look somewhat like a curve.

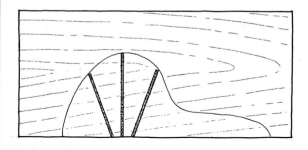

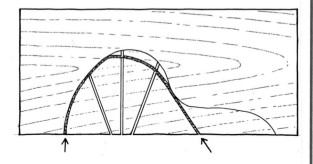

1. Make relief cuts in the tightest part of the curve.

2. Cut one side of the curve until the blade nears the line.

3. Cut the other side of the curve in the same way.

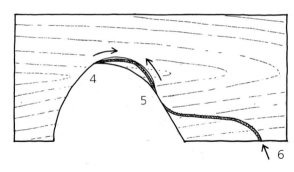

4. Move the piece so the side of the blade touches the curve near the top, then saw as close to the line as you can.

5. Saw as close to the line as you can.

6. Saw this line to complete the pattern.

The finished curve is somewhat choppy—not nearly as good as if the proper-width blade were used in the first place.

Nesting Parts to Reduce Waste

Sawing curved parts generates a lot of waste. I know this firsthand because I specialize in building 18th-century furniture such as Queen Anne and Chippendale. The chair leg in the photo at right is a good example. During the creation of the graceful curved legs for the back of a chair, several small, irregularly shaped blocks are produced. Although I often find a use for some of the larger offcuts, much of it goes into the wood stove.

To avoid generating so much waste, I nest pieces together whenever I can (see the drawing below). By selecting a board wide enough for two, three, or even four legs, I can substantially reduce the amount of waste.

By using a pattern and nesting the pieces, the rear legs of this Chippendale chair can be nested and sawn from one board to avoid waste.

You can reduce waste substantially by nesting parts together. Here, I've used a plywood pattern to draw two nested sets of Chippendale chair rear legs on one wide board.

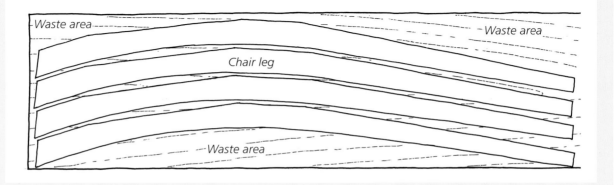

Waste area

Waste area

Chair leg

Waste area

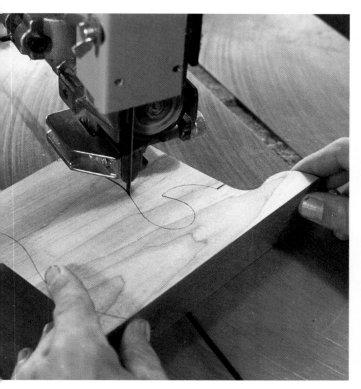

Grasping the work on rear corners provides good control in most situations.

Grasping the work on diagonal corners provides good control and, in this case, keeps fingers out of the blade's path.

but I don't like it because it results in choppy, angular curves instead of smooth, flowing ones. It's better to take the time to change the blade if it is too wide for the radius of the curve.

Hand position

When sawing curves on your bandsaw, hand position is important both for control and for safety. Spacing your hands far apart gives the most control. Using this technique, you can use one hand to push the workpiece and the other hand to steer or guide the work. I've found that for most pieces I'm sawing, it works well to hold the rear adjacent corners (see the left photo above) or diagonal corners (see the right photo above). Either of these hand positions allows me to easily follow the twists, turns, and scrolls of even the most intricate curves.

As I follow the line, I'm also keenly aware of the position of my hands in relation to the blade. To avoid coming in contact with the blade, it's often necessary to change hand positions in the middle or near the end of the cut.

On long, narrow work such as this chair leg, you gain the most control by grasping the workpiece near the ends.

When sawing long, gentle curves such as those found on a chair leg, I normally grip each end of the stock (see the photo above). Because I'm right-handed, I feel most comfortable using my right hand primarily for pushing the stock and my left hand for steering.

Stacking Multiples

You can save considerable time on sawing by stacking multiple pieces and sawing them together (see the photos on the facing page). It's important to keep the parts aligned so that they remain identical. Masking tape works well for this job. I stack the parts and bind them together tightly with a couple of layers of tape. Once the pieces are wrapped, I mark the layout on the top piece directly on the tape.

After I've completed sawing, I leave the pieces stacked while I smooth the sawmarks from the edges. It may be necessary to add another layer of tape if much of the original tape was cut when sawing.

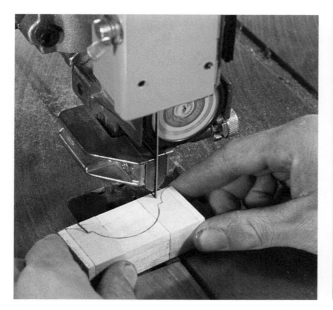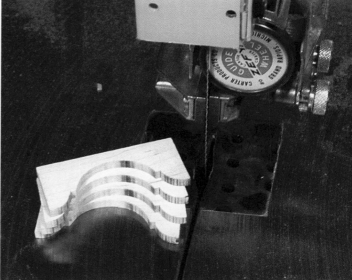

You can save time by stacking multiples and sawing them together. To keep them aligned when sawing, tape them together with masking tape.

Blade pitch for stacks

Be sure to select a blade pitch for the combined thickness of the pieces you're cutting.

Once you've tried this method a couple of times, I'm sure you'll appreciate the time it saves not only in sawing but also in layout since you won't have to draw the lines on each individual piece.

It's important to realize that there are limits to the number of pieces that you can safely and accurately stack. The higher you raise the guidepost to accommodate a tall stack, the less support the blade has from the upper guide. As a result, the blade may deflect and cause the lowest pieces in the stack to be miscut. Because you're following the layout on the top piece, you'll be unaware that the pieces underneath are being miscut. To minimize this problem, first tension the blade properly and adjust the guides. Then make a test cut to determine how tall a stack you can accurately cut through the twists and turns of your design.

Limits to stacking

For your safety, it is important for a stack to have a substantial footprint. Otherwise, the sawblade can grab it violently, causing you to lose control. Don't stack small pieces together in a tall tower. As a general rule, the height of a stack should be no more than its width.

Ripping on the Bandsaw

If you own a table saw, you may wonder why you would want to rip stock on a bandsaw. Isn't the table saw the best choice for ripping stock? Not always. A bandsaw has several definite advantages over a table saw when it comes to ripping, especially if the stock is very thick or warped.

The main advantage of ripping on a bandsaw is safety. Table saws can kick back violently, but a bandsaw can't kick back because the blade pushes the stock downward toward the table. Ripping stock that is twisted or warped in any way poses an even greater risk on the table saw because warped stock is more prone to binding the blade, which almost always results in kickback. Without a doubt, ripping on a bandsaw is safer.

Another advantage to ripping on a bandsaw is that it rips faster than a table saw and with half as much waste. The reason for this is simple: A bandsaw blade is thin, so it produces a narrow kerf. In fact, the typical bandsaw blade produces a kerf that is half that of a table-saw kerf (see the photo below). This results in less feed resistance, which makes ripping faster, especially when ripping thick hardwood. As a bonus, you'll get greater yield from your expensive stock.

Selecting a blade for ripping

Your best blade for ripping is one with a coarse pitch that places no more than six teeth in contact with the stock at one time. For example, if you're ripping 2-in.-thick stock, a 3-pitch blade would be ideal. The large gullets in a coarse-pitch blade will keep the kerf cleared of sawdust. Also, I prefer a blade with hook teeth for ripping. The aggressive cutting action of hook teeth creates very little feed resistance. In fact, hook teeth seem to almost feed themselves. To prevent blade deflection and drift, I suggest using the widest blade that will fit on your bandsaw. See chapter 6 for more information on choosing and tensioning a blade.

Freehand ripping vs. ripping with a fence

Freehand ripping simply means that you don't use a fence to guide the stock (see the photo at left on the facing page). Just mark a straight line as a guide and follow it while ripping the stock. Freehand rip-

A bandsaw kerf (left) is half the width of a table-saw kerf (right).

ping is fast because it doesn't involve setting a fence, so I often rip freehand when I've only got a couple of pieces of stock. Freehand ripping is also my choice when the stock is warped because there is no chance of it binding on a fence.

Ripping with a fence yields more consistent dimensions than ripping freehand. Whenever accuracy is required, I use a simple fence. It's also faster when there is a lot of stock to be ripped because you don't have to mark each piece with a straight line.

You may have to adjust your fence to compensate for blade drift. Blade drift simply means that the blade isn't cutting parallel to the table edge. If you attempt to rip without compensating for drift, the stock may wander from the fence, causing the stock to be cut undersized.

Many factory-made fences won't work for ripping because they are made to lock parallel to

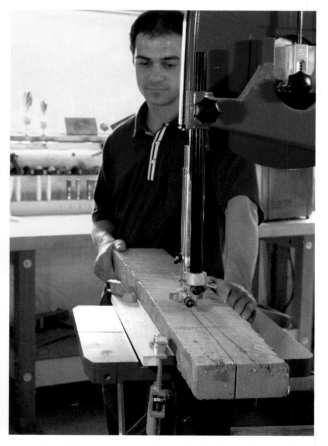

> ## Blade drift and narrow blades
>
> I've noticed that blade drift is only a problem with blades that are ½ in. or less in width. In my experience, blades that are 1 in. or wider typically rip parallel to the fence.

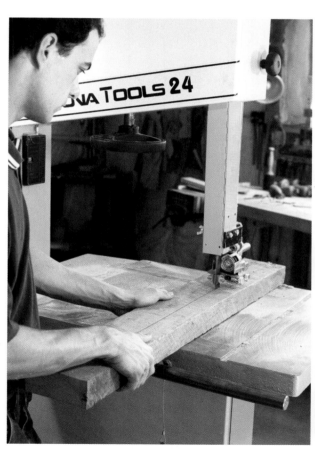

You don't need a fence when ripping on the bandsaw, just a straight line and a steady eye.

Any straight strip of wood is suitable for a fence when ripping, but you'll have to set it to take blade drift into account.

Setting the Fence for Blade Drift

The degree of drift for each blade will be a little different, so you'll have to check for drift each time you change blades. Fortunately, finding the blade-drift angle is easy.

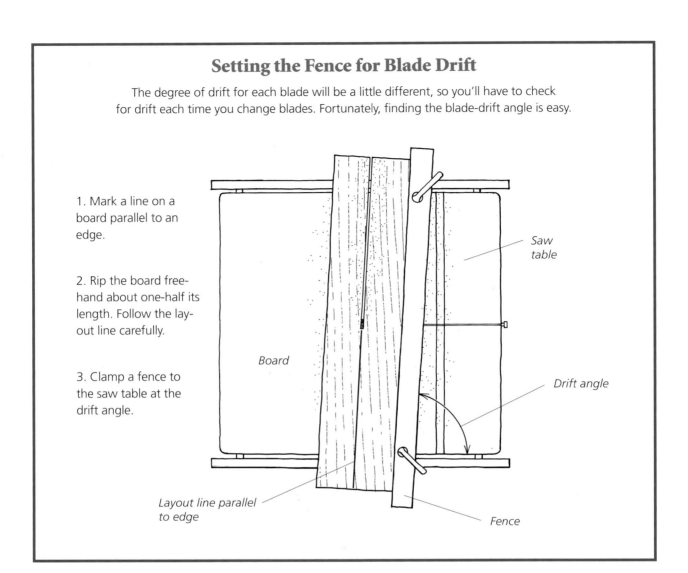

1. Mark a line on a board parallel to an edge.

2. Rip the board free-hand about one-half its length. Follow the lay-out line carefully.

3. Clamp a fence to the saw table at the drift angle.

Board

Saw table

Drift angle

Layout line parallel to edge

Fence

Use a push stick
A bandsaw may be a relatively safe tool, but always use a push stick when ripping narrow stock.

the table edge. If your fence doesn't have an adjustment for drift, then you can make your own fence that clamps to the saw table. If you're in a hurry, a board with one true edge or a strip of ¾-in. plywood will suffice. Just make certain that your fence is clamped securely to the table.

Hand position
When ripping freehand, I use my right hand for pushing and both hands for guiding the stock. When ripping with a fence, I push with my right hand and hold the stock against the fence with my left hand. It's important to keep both hands a safe distance from the blade and finish the cut with a push stick.

Removing Bandsaw Marks

Unfortunately, bandsaws don't create finished surfaces, so after bandsawing, you'll have to smooth away the sawmarks from the surface. This can be done in a number of ways, such as by filing, by sanding, or even by cutting away the bandsawn surface with a router or shaper.

The more accurately you saw to the layout line, the less cleanup is required. Careless bandsawing leaves the sawn surface bumpy, and you'll have to remove more than just sawmarks. You'll have to remove enough wood to create a smooth, flowing curve. Creating the curve by hand with a file is much more labor-intensive than creating the curve on a bandsaw, so it's important to saw accurately.

Files

Small files are indispensable for removing sawmarks, especially in small, difficult-to-reach areas. Half-round files, as the name implies, are curved on one face and flat on the opposite face. Round files are available to fit the smallest of contours.

Spindle sanders

Using a spindle sander is one of the fastest and easiest ways to smooth a bandsawn contour (see the photo at left on p. 128). Most spindle sanders have at least a half dozen sanding drums of different diameters to accommodate the radius of the curve you're working.

Floor-model spindle sanders are the most powerful and come with the widest

You can avoid tedious smoothing of curved parts by sawing precisely to the layout line.

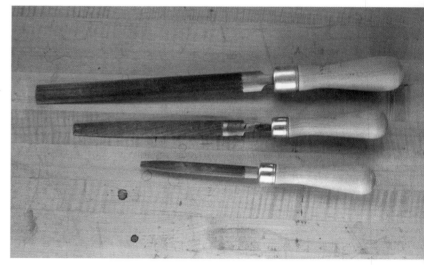

Files are indispensable tools for removing bandsaw marks. They come in a variety of shapes to suit almost any curve.

A spindle sander will make quick work of smoothing concave areas of curved work.

When the work is to be template routed, I'm not as fussy about sawing to the line.

assortment of sanding drums. On the other hand, small benchtop sanders are more affordable. The best benchtop sanders are industrial-quality machines that are powerful enough for any job.

Carving gouges and chisels

If you enjoy making reproductions of colonial American furniture, then you may wish to use carving gouges to remove the bandsaw marks from your work. Eighteenth-century craftsmen used gouges of various sizes and sweeps (radii of the curves) to carve away sawmarks and create flowing contours on their work. Wherever gouges were used to carve away the inside edges of a chair rail or table apron, craftsmen would chamfer the edges afterwards.

As you might imagine, this can be a time-consuming method that you may wish to use only when you're attempting to strictly reproduce an antique. Although I seldom use this method, I do use ordinary flat chisels quite often to create crisp inside corners on my bandsawn work.

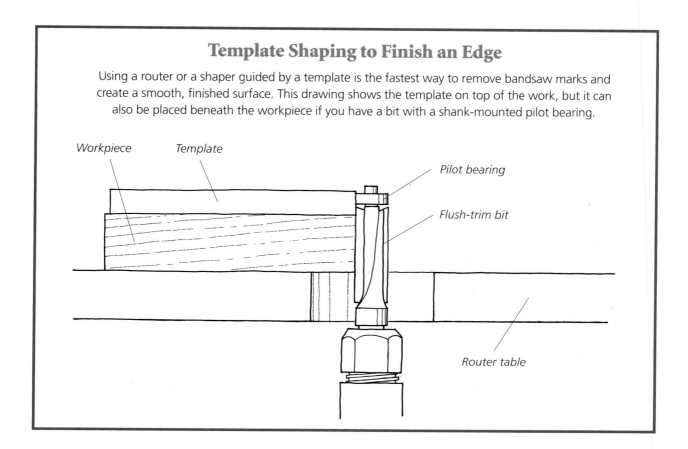

Template Shaping to Finish an Edge

Using a router or a shaper guided by a template is the fastest way to remove bandsaw marks and create a smooth, finished surface. This drawing shows the template on top of the work, but it can also be placed beneath the workpiece if you have a bit with a shank-mounted pilot bearing.

Workpiece

Template

Pilot bearing

Flush-trim bit

Router table

Template shaping

As I mentioned earlier, you generally want to follow the layout line as closely as possible when sawing contours. By carefully following the line, you can avoid the tedious cleanup associated with careless sawing. But there are times when you can saw "heavy" of the line and make the final, exact contour with a router or a shaper.

The technique is called template shaping, and it's a fast, easy way to reproduce an exact contour in any number of pieces of stock. Because a router or a shaper produces the final surface, it's not impor-

tant to saw exactly to the layout line. In this case, a bandsaw is used to remove the excess stock before making the finished cut with a router or a shaper.

To use this technique, you'll first have to make a template, which must be the exact contour that you want to reproduce. Next, secure the stock to the template with toggle clamps, brads, or double-sided tape. Before shaping, select a router bit or shaper cutter with the desired profile. The bit or cutter must have a bearing to follow the contours of the template (see the drawing above).

Using a template-guided router or shaper is the fastest way to remove bandsaw marks from curved stock.

Once you've got a good template, removing bandsaw marks with this method is remarkably fast and easy. As the bearing on the router or shaper follows the template, the cutter removes the bandsaw marks and creates an exact copy of the template contour on the workpiece.

I use my table-mounted router for small- and medium-size cuts, and my shaper for large, heavy cuts. Although this is a great technique, it does have a few limitations. First, neither a router nor a shaper can create sharp inside corners (see the bottom photo at left). To solve this problem, you can either soften the inside corner to accommodate the bearing diameter, or you can do what I do: Shape as much as possible, then carve inside corners by hand. The radius of a contour that you wish to shape must be no smaller than the bearing diameter. This is where a router bit has a distinct advantage over a shaper cutter; its small bearing will turn through a much tighter curve.

Removing marks on ripped boards

When ripping straight stock on a bandsaw, you'll also want to remove the bandsaw marks and create a finished surface. Either a jointer, a planer, or a handplane will work.

The lower piece shows the best a router can do to shape an inside corner. I've carved the correct profile into the upper piece by hand.

Advanced Bandsaw Techniques

The bandsaw is a highly versatile machine capable of much more than basic curves. For example, by cutting stock on two faces, you can create compound curves such as cabriole legs and ogee feet. You can resaw wide boards straight through or on a curve. With the right blade and a precision tune-up, your bandsaw can also cut fine joinery. You can even use a template to make multiples of a complex curved piece.

In this chapter, I'll cover these topics as well methods for slicing your own veneer. So read on to discover ways to broaden the scope of your next woodworking project.

Compound Curves

A compound curve is one that flows in two directions simultaneously. When it comes to compound curves in furniture, probably the best-known example is the cabriole leg, as shown in the photo at right on p. 132. The curves on a cabriole leg begin at the top of the leg, or knee, taper gracefully downward toward the slender ankle, then quickly broaden again at the foot. Another common example is the ogee bracket foot. I tend to talk about 18th-century furniture, which is what I specialize in building, but compound curves are also found in the stylized forms of legs used on many contemporary furniture designs.

You can use your bandsaw to make compound curves such as those found on this ogee foot. Here, the basic outline has been cut, and the operator is now sawing the curve in one of the outside edges.

The cabriole legs on this Chippendale chair are a perfect example of compound curves—they curve in two directions at the same time.

Although cutting compound curves may seem intimidating, it is easy to do with your bandsaw. It simply involves sawing curves on two adjacent surfaces.

As with all curves, begin by sketching a design on thin plywood and bandsawing the pattern. Most likely you'll have to do some smoothing of the curves of the pattern with a file—I usually do. Next, trace the pattern outline onto two adjacent faces of the stock. After bandsawing the first face, rotate the stock 90° and saw the second face. It's that easy. Afterwards, you'll have to use hand tools to connect and blend the curves.

If you've always wanted to make furniture with compound curves, then I encourage you to give it a try. It's surprisingly easy, and it's exciting to see a straight, square blank of wood so quickly transformed. I'll now cover the process step-by-step, so read on to discover how

Take time to get the pattern right

It's important to take time to make sure that the curves of your pattern are smooth and flowing because any flaws in the pattern will be transferred to the workpiece and duplicated.

When enlarging a curve, draw it first, then glue the paper pattern directly to the plywood pattern stock before bandsawing.

you can add compound curves to your next project.

Cabriole legs

As the first example of how to make a compound curve, I'll use a cabriole leg. Legs always come in pairs, so you'll need a pattern to duplicate the curves. I like to use ¼-in. birch plywood for patterns. It's strong, stiff, and the edges don't fray and wear away as will cardboard or paper.

Drawing a curved leg is actually more difficult than sawing and sculpting it. Good proportions between the knee, ankle, and foot are critical. If this is your first time, I suggest you use one of the patterns I've provided, such as the cabriole leg for the Connecticut Tea Table on pp. 176-177. You can enlarge the drawing by redrawing the grid full size, plotting the points, and sketching in the curve, or you can have it done at a copy shop. Once you've enlarged the drawing, glue it to the plywood (see the photo above). I use rubber cement to prevent the paper from wrinkling. Carefully bandsaw the pattern along the layout lines, as shown in the photo at right. After sawing, smooth the

edges with a file. While filing, look for irregularities in the curve, and make sure the curve has smooth, flowing lines.

Laying out the leg When milling the stock for a cabriole leg, I size it approximately ¹⁄₁₆ in. larger all around than the pattern. This allows me to easily follow the contours of the pattern when I trace

Accurately sawing to the line

Saw right next to the line so that the blade teeth touch the line but the kerf falls in the waste.

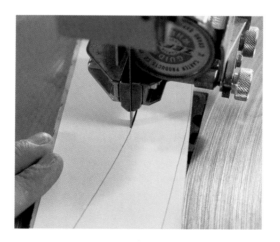

Accurate cutting reduces the amount of filing and sanding you'll do later to get the curve smooth.

Trace the cabriole leg pattern onto two adjacent faces of the leg stock back-to-back rather than knee-to-knee so you can cut the joints while the stock is still square.

around it. There's a lot of waste in a cabriole leg, so I examine the stock for minor defects, such as small knots or tearout, and locate them in the waste.

After you've traced the pattern onto the first surface, turn the leg to the adjacent surface and trace it a second time. I orient the pattern back-to-back rather than knee-to-knee. This way I can locate the area of the leg post and lay out and cut the mortise while the leg is still square.

If the leg is somewhat longer than the table on my bandsaw, I leave a couple of areas square when sawing the first face to support the leg on the table when cutting the adjacent face (see the drawing below). I'll refer to these areas as bridges. When I've finished sawing, I cut the bridges away. After sawing the first face, save the offcut at the back of the leg because it has the drawing for the adjacent face. I reattach the offcut with masking tape before sawing the adjacent face.

Bandsawing the leg Before bandsawing, make sure you have the right blade on your machine. For a typical cabriole leg, I choose a ¼-in.-wide, 6-pitch, regular-tooth blade. This narrow blade enables me to navigate the tight contour of the ankle.

Begin by making short, straight preliminary cuts for the bridges that support the second face and also at the inside corner where the knee adjoins the post (see the photo at left on the facing page). These cuts are easy to back out of, and they allow

Bridges Support the Leg while Cutting

When you are sawing a cabriole leg, bridges support the leg during the second cut. After completing the second cut, saw off the bridges.

Rotate the stock 90° to make the second cut.

Cut this line first.

Bridges

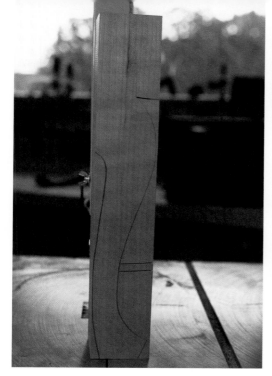

My first sawcuts are the short, straight relief cuts at the knee and bridge.

You'll have to tape this offcut back into position before sawing the second face.

you to avoid trapping the blade at the end of a long curve.

Next, start at the foot and saw the leg contours. As you approach each intersection where you made the preliminary cuts, reduce the feed pressure and ease into the junction. After sawing the contour at the back of the leg, save the offcut and tape it back into position (see the top right photo). Sawing the adjacent face is a repeat of what you've just done. When you're finished, you can saw off the existing bridges from the leg.

The sawn leg will have a graceful, curved but somewhat square appearance (see the top photo on p. 136). Use rasps and files to round the corners and blend

The bridges support the leg while sawing the second face.

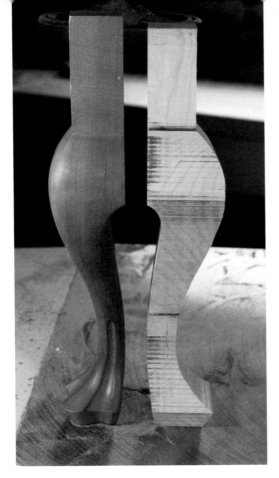

After band-sawing, use rasps and files to shape and smooth the leg.

the four leg surfaces. For more details on shaping the leg, see chapter 10.

Ogee bracket feet

Like a cabriole leg, the surfaces of an ogee foot are flowing compound curves. An ogee foot even has the classic cyma, or S, curve. It's commonly used to support casework such as chests and desks on many different styles of furniture.

But whereas a cabriole leg is sawn from a piece of solid stock, an ogee foot is sawn from two pieces joined at a right angle, typically with a miter reinforced with a spline (see the photo on the facing page).

Just as with a cabriole leg, you begin by drawing a pattern. You should realize, however, that you'll need a pattern that includes both the bracket outline and the ogee contour on the face of the foot (see the drawing on the facing page). Ogee feet come in many sizes to fit small chests to large, full-scale casework.

Cutting the joint Begin by cutting the miter joint that joins the two parts of the foot. I should mention that feet at the rear of a case have the ogee contour only at the side where it may be seen. The portion of the foot at the back of the case where it isn't usually seen is simply a square board that is fastened to the ogee half of the foot with half-blind dovetails (see the drawing on p. 138).

Before gluing the two halves of the foot together, bandsaw the bracket profile. The

Like the cabriole leg, the ogee foot has flowing curves on adjacent faces.

The two halves of a bracket foot are glued with a miter and plywood spline.

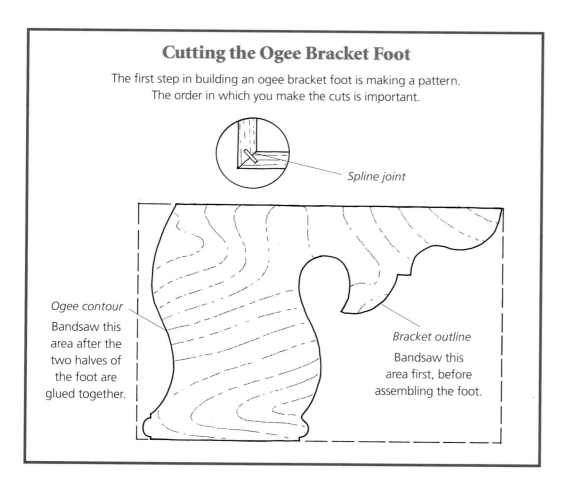

Cutting the Ogee Bracket Foot

The first step in building an ogee bracket foot is making a pattern.
The order in which you make the cuts is important.

Spline joint

Ogee contour
Bandsaw this area after the two halves of the foot are glued together.

Bracket outline
Bandsaw this area first, before assembling the foot.

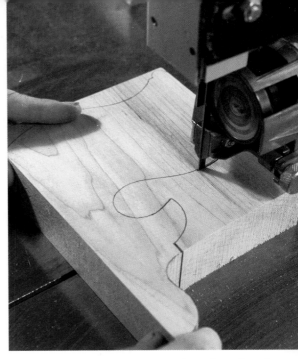

Ogee Foot at the Back of the Casework

The feet at the back of the piece, which typically aren't seen, are not made with an elaborate scroll. Instead they are simple brackets fastened to the ogee half of the foot with half-blind dovetails.

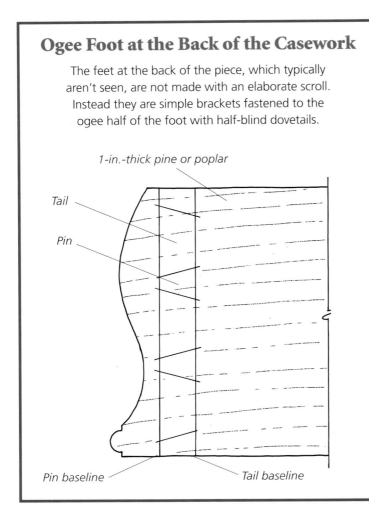

1-in.-thick pine or poplar

Tail

Pin

Pin baseline

Tail baseline

Before gluing the two halves of the foot, bandsaw the bracket outline.

You can leave some sawmarks

It's really not necessary to smooth away all of the sawmarks inside the bracket area of the foot because they won't be seen once the finished foot is fastened to the base of the casework.

profile is often a combination of tight contours, so I use a narrow ³⁄₁₆-in. or ⅛-in. blade. The photo on the facing page shows the proper sequence of cuts. Next, smooth the sawn surfaces with a file or a spindle sander.

Bandsawing the ogee profile Before you begin sawing, you'll need to build a stand to support the foot as it is being sawn. The stand I use is stone simple. I fasten four boards together with dadoes, glue, and screws (see the drawing on the facing page). The stand doesn't have to be fancy—just sturdy and tall enough to suspend the foot off of the bandsaw table and position it parallel to the blade.

Now you're ready to begin sawing the foot. Secure the foot to the stand with a small clamp and adjust the upper guide no more than ¼ in. above the work for maximum safety and blade support.

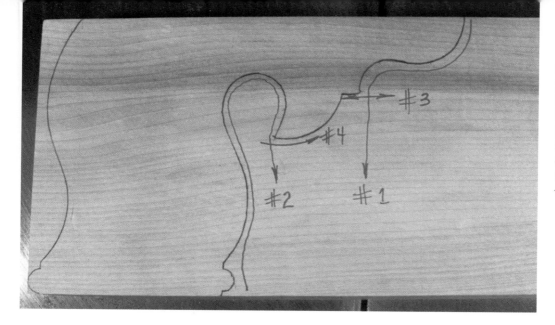

In a complex pattern such as this, it's important to plan your sequence of cuts so the blade won't get trapped.

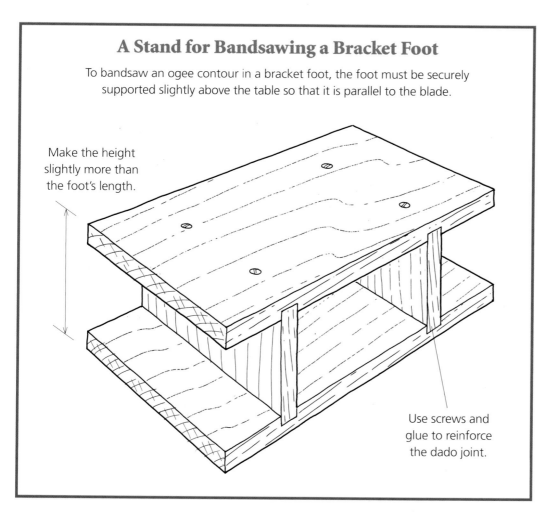

A Stand for Bandsawing a Bracket Foot

To bandsaw an ogee contour in a bracket foot, the foot must be securely supported slightly above the table so that it is parallel to the blade.

Make the height slightly more than the foot's length.

Use screws and glue to reinforce the dado joint.

The foot is supported on a simple stand for bandsawing the ogee contour into the face.

Feed slowly and cut close to the line. It will save a lot of time hand-shaping later.

The outline of the second face is revealed by the miter joint.

> ### Blade for sawing an ogee bracket foot
>
> A ¼-in., 4-pitch blade works well for the foot pattern I've provided. Proper tension is important to prevent the blade from deflecting and spoiling the foot.

Feed the workpiece slowly while sawing the foot, and follow the layout line as accurately as possible. This gives the foot a smooth, flowing contour and saves a lot of extra shaping by hand. When the first side is complete, reposition the foot and bandsaw the second face. You won't need to tape the offcut back in place for the layout line. You'll see that the foot contour for the second face is outlined by the miter joint (see the bottom photo on the facing page). When you're finished sawing the foot, clean it up in the usual way with files. You can also use a sharp rabbet plane for the square shoulders on either side of the bead.

Resawing

Resawing is the process of ripping a board through its thickness to make thinner boards. If you're making small boxes of any type, such as drawers, humidors, or jewelry boxes, you will need thin lumber. Rather than planing away excess thickness, you can resaw the stock and reduce your lumber expenses.

Probably the greatest benefit of resawing is that it gives you the ability to create your own veneer. With the right blade and a well-tuned bandsaw, you can create veneer as thin as $\frac{1}{16}$ in.

Using veneer is a dramatic way to decorate small boxes or to create a set of matching drawer fronts for a chest or desk. Whenever I come across a board that is highly figured, such as a walnut crotch or a slab of tight-grained curly maple, I set it aside for use as veneer. If you've never sawn your own veneer, I encourage you to give it a try. Using figured veneer is an exciting way to add visual appeal to almost any woodworking project.

Choosing a blade

More than any other bandsaw operation, resawing requires the right blade, and it must be sharp. A coarse-pitch blade is critical for sawing thin, consistently uni-

A well-tuned bandsaw can slice veneer from wide figured stock such as this walnut board.

Book-matched veneer sawn on your own bandsaw is a great way to add distinction to your work.

form veneer. Otherwise, the gullets pack with sawdust, and the blade bows and spoils your lumber. I prefer a variable-pitch hook-tooth blade, such as a 2/3 pitch, because it creates a smoother surface by limiting harmonic vibrations. Also, the hook-style tooth is very aggressive, which minimizes feed resistance.

For additional smoothness, it's tough to beat carbide. The carbide-tipped blades I have for my bandsaw produce a surface so smooth that very little sanding is required. This is a distinct advantage when sawing veneer.

Blade width is important, too. I recommend that you use the widest blade that your saw can properly tension. For woodworkers with a 14-in. bandsaw, that means a ½-in. blade.

Setting tension and guides

As I pointed out in chapter 4, a bandsaw blade requires 25,000 psi for maximum beam strength to resist deflection. When resawing, you definitely need this much tension. I use a tension meter to accurately tension the blade in preparation for resawing. If you have a 14-in. bandsaw and don't own a tension meter, then I recommend that you tension the blade until the tension spring is nearly compressed.

Guide adjustment is another key to produc-

ing thin, uniform sheets of veneer. You'll want to set each guide to within 0.003 in. of the blade. If you have block guides, check them for wear, and if necessary, true the faces with a file. The thrust wheel must be set close as well. I've found that guide adjustment is never more critical than with resawing. For more detail on guide adjustments, see pp. 99-102.

Using a resaw fence

Most bandsaw blades suffer from a phenomenon called drift, which means that the blades don't rip in a line that is parallel to the fence. Obviously, this can be a problem if you attempt to use your bandsaw fence to guide the stock. In my experience, the worst offenders are blades that are ½ in. wide or less. I've found that wide blades, such as 1 in. or 1¼ in., will rip parallel to the fence. So if you have a large bandsaw that can handle wide blades, you can probably use the fence that came with your saw. Otherwise, I recommend that you construct a simple plywood fence for your bandsaw so you can position it at the angle of drift (see pp. 125-126). See p. 163 for more information on how to build a resaw fence. Once the blade is tensioned and the fence is in place, make a test cut to double-check the final stock thickness.

Making the cut

Although resawing veneer takes a little practice, it's really quite easy to develop a feel for the technique. I recommend that you begin by feeding the plank very slowly, then gradually increasing the feed rate. If you're sensitive to the sounds and vibrations that the saw is producing, you'll

When bandsawing veneer, feed the stock slowly and be attentive to the sounds of your bandsaw. You'll know when you're feeding the stock too fast by the sound.

Sawing shallow kerfs first with your table saw makes resawing quick and easy, although it's not as precise as using a fence.

know when you're pushing the machine too hard. Remember to save your fingers by finishing the cut with a push stick.

Resawing without a fence

Another method for resawing on a bandsaw doesn't use a fence, but it does require a table saw. First, rip shallow kerfs on the edges of the stock with the table saw, then finish the cuts on the bandsaw—without a fence (see the right photo above). A sharp blade will have a natural tendency to follow the path of least resistance, which

is along the kerfs from the table saw. I use this method when my concern is speed rather than precision. In that case, I don't

Resaw fences are high

Height is important on a resaw fence so that wide boards are well supported. If your bandsaw came with a decent fence, consider screwing or bolting a high plywood face to it. If you're building your own fence, it's easy to make it high enough for wide boards.

want or need to take the time to set the fence and guides precisely.

Resawing on a curve

Another useful bandsaw technique to know is how to resaw a curve. Many furniture parts, such as the back of the chair on p. 132, have wide, curved parts that are relatively thin. A straight fence is useless for guiding curved stock, yet it is impossible to accurately cut such an awkward piece freehand.

The key to resawing a curve accurately is to use a point fence. This is simply a narrow piece of wood with a chamfered point that mounts to the resaw fence parallel to and right at the blade. The point fence guides the stock and positions it parallel to the blade, yet it allows you to pivot the stock to follow the contoured outline.

To use a point fence, mark the layout of the curve on the edge of the stock. Then bandsaw the first face freehand without the fence, carefully following the layout line (see the photo at left). Before sawing the second face, remove the bandsaw marks with a spokeshave to smooth the surface and create a flowing curve (see the photo at left on the facing page).

Next, lay out a parallel curved line to indicate the final thickness of the workpiece. For accurate results, I use a sharp marking gauge and follow the first curve (see the top photo at right on the facing page). Before bandsawing the second

To resaw a curve, you must first saw one face freehand. Carefully follow the layout line.

Use a sharp spokeshave to remove the bandsaw marks from the curved face and to smooth the curve.

Use a marking gauge to scribe the second face parallel to the first.

curve, fasten the point fence adjacent to the teeth of the blade at a distance equal to the final thickness.

To make the final cut, position the smooth, contoured face of the stock against the point fence and begin sawing (see the photo at right). As you saw, press the stock firmly against the fence, and pivot the stock to follow the scribed layout line from the marking gauge. Overfeeding can cause the blade to deflect, so feed the stock slowly and pay attention to the sounds and vibrations produced by your bandsaw.

Hold the workpiece firmly to the point fence and pivot it to follow the layout line to cut the second face.

Bandsaw Joinery

Because table saws are good at making accurate, square joints, it's natural that most woodworkers think first of a table saw for making joints, especially tenons. But you can also achieve surprisingly accurate work with your bandsaw. And if you don't own a table saw, then your bandsaw is certainly a good option.

For cutting joints such as dovetails and tenons on your bandsaw, you'll need a precision blade and guides to control the cut. You'll also want to review chapter 6 and make sure your saw is properly tuned. If the blade is bouncing or vibrating excessively, you can't expect to execute precise joinery. It's also vital that the table is 90° to the blade when cutting tenons and that the miter gauge is adjusted to cut square.

The best choice for a joinery blade is one that is wide with a fine pitch. The extra blade width will help to ensure that the blade cuts straight without wandering. A ½-in. blade works well for this application. The fine pitch will create the smooth surface needed for a snug fit inside the joint and a good glue bond.

When you're ready to saw, guide the stock through your bandsaw just as you would on a table saw: by using the fence and the miter gauge. To create the angles necessary for dovetails, you'll have to tilt the table to the left. I use a 15° angle for dovetails, but if your bandsaw table doesn't tilt that far, you can either use a smaller angle, such as 10°, or you can build an auxiliary angled table that clamps to your bandsaw's table (as shown in the drawing on p. 150).

Mortise-and-tenon joinery

The mortise-and-tenon joint is the strongest method for joining two pieces of wood end to edge to form a right angle. I use the mortise-and-tenon joint for making face frames on furniture and cabinets as well as for the frames on frame-

The Mortise-and-Tenon Joint

The mortise-and-tenon joint is the strongest way to join two pieces of wood at a right angle. Cut the mortise first, then the tenon to fit.

Mortise

Tenon face

Tenon shoulder

and-panel doors. I always cut the mortise first, then I cut the tenon to fit. Although I use a hollow-chisel mortising machine to cut the mortise, a plunge router also works well.

For a joint to be strong, the tenon must fit snugly inside the mortise. A standard tenon has four surfaces: two shoulders that bear against the outside of the mortise, and two tenon faces that fit within the walls of the mortise.

Cutting a tenon on the bandsaw involves sawing the shoulders first, then the two faces. Layout is critical to well-fitting joints. I use a knife and a marking gauge to incise the wood fibers for a clean cut and to help avoid confusion about which part of the stock is to be sawn away. I encourage you to take care to mill the stock precisely. Each piece must be identical in thickness, width, and length for a consistent fit of the joints.

After layout, the next step is to cut the shoulders. First, position a test piece in front of the blade for the cut. If I'm making only one or two tenons, I cut free-hand, but if I'm making several tenons, I use stops. Stops greatly increase accuracy and efficiency when cutting multiple pieces of stock. To create a fixed distance between the end of the tenon and the shoulder, use the fence as a stop. Use a second stop to control the depth of the shoulder.

Use the miter gauge to cut the tenon shoulders.

Mill all stock at once
Whenever I'm working wood to precise tolerances with a machine, I find that it's crucial to mill all the stock together along with a test piece. This helps to ensure both accuracy and consistency between all pieces of stock.

After the tenon shoulders are cut, set the fence to guide the workpiece for cutting the tenon face. This is when a test piece of stock is especially helpful. I hold the stock against the fence in front of the blade and bring the fence and test piece

Use the layout lines as a guide when setting the fence.

Fitting the tenon

Slight fence adjustments may yield significant changes in the tenon thickness because each cut must be made on both faces of the stock to keep the tenon centered.

As you slice the face of each tenon, press the stock firmly against the fence.

A mortise-and-tenon joint is extremely strong but only when the pieces fit together snugly.

toward the blade until the teeth are right on the layout line, then I lock the fence in place. A block of wood clamped to the rear portion of the fence will act as a stop and ensure that each tenon is the same length.

Now you're ready to make the test cuts on both sides of the tenon and to test the fit within the mortise. The indication of a proper fit is when the tenon is snug within the mortise yet it doesn't require heavy blows from a mallet to assemble. If the fit isn't just right, it's easy to make adjustments by moving the fence and making more test cuts.

Dovetail joinery

No other woodworking joint denotes quality quite like the dovetail. Like the mortise-and-tenon joint, the dovetail has been around for centuries. And although faster methods of joinery have been devised, no other joint comes close to the strength of the dovetail's interlocking tails and pins.

The dovetail joint has a look of excellence when well executed, but it can be a distracting eyesore if poorly done. Unfortunately, cutting the joint by hand requires a high degree of skill and confidence. I don't think that router jigs are a viable alternative to hand-cutting dove-

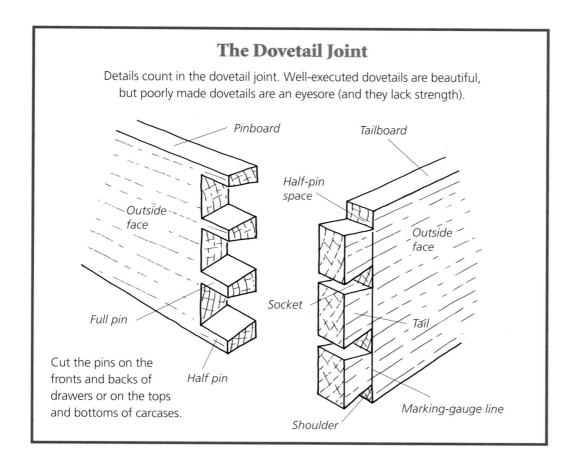

The Dovetail Joint

Details count in the dovetail joint. Well-executed dovetails are beautiful, but poorly made dovetails are an eyesore (and they lack strength).

Pinboard

Tailboard

Half-pin space

Outside face

Outside face

Full pin

Socket

Tail

Half pin

Marking-gauge line

Cut the pins on the fronts and backs of drawers or on the tops and bottoms of carcases.

Shoulder

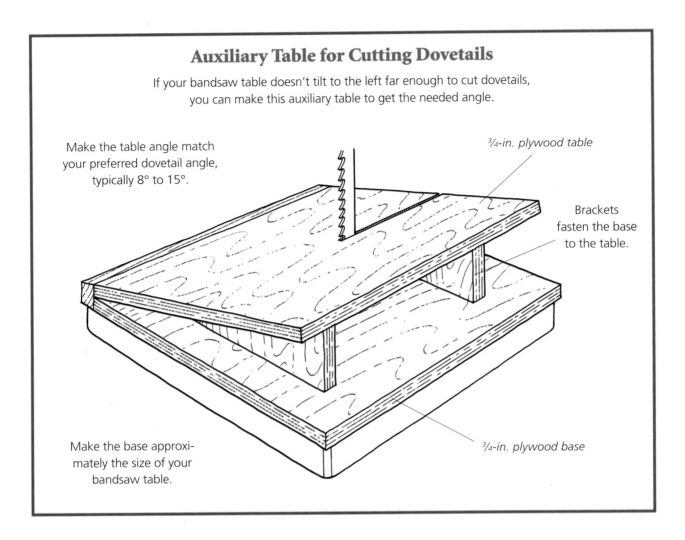

Auxiliary Table for Cutting Dovetails

If your bandsaw table doesn't tilt to the left far enough to cut dovetails,
you can make this auxiliary table to get the needed angle.

Make the table angle match
your preferred dovetail angle,
typically 8° to 15°.

¾-in. plywood table

Brackets
fasten the base
to the table.

Make the base approxi-
mately the size of your
bandsaw table.

¾-in. plywood base

tails because to my eye the completed joint has a machine-made, inferior look. Also, many of the router jigs I've seen cut both boards at once. They are complicated to set up, and if one of the many adjustments isn't quite right, then both the pinboard and the tailboard are spoiled.

Although I cut dovetails by hand, as a woodworking instructor I've become sympathetic to those who lack the time or patience to practice making the joint. An

excellent alternative is to cut half of the joint with a bandsaw and cut the second half by hand to fit. Most people who I introduce to this technique find that it doesn't require nearly as much time to learn, and there's very little measuring or layout involved. Also, since the pinboard is made first on the bandsaw and the tailboard is cut to match the pinboard, you don't lose all of your work if you make a mistake on one of them. Best of all, this technique yields a handmade look because you can control the size and spacing of the joint's tails and pins, which you cannot do on a router jig.

All you need to cut dovetails on a bandsaw is a saw with a table that tilts both to the right and to the left up to 15°. If your bandsaw table doesn't tilt both ways, you can still cut dovetails using the auxiliary table shown in the drawing on the facing page.

For your first set of bandsaw dovetails, I suggest you start with a simple arrangement: one full pin and two half pins. This looks good when made in fairly narrow workpieces, such as drawer sides or shallow boxes.

One way to cut dovetails on a bandsaw is to draw the pins on a board with the spacing you want and simply saw them out. Just tilt the table and adjust the fence until the blade aligns with the marks. Reset the fence for each cut, and tilt the table in the opposite direction to get the other side of the pins (see the bottom photo at right). This simple method is how I most often use a bandsaw for dovetails.

There's another method that requires very little measurement and no laying out or making marks on the end grain. It uses nothing more complicated than spacer blocks and a fence (see the drawing on pp. 152-153). The bandsaw setup takes care of everything. All you need to know is the width of your workpiece and the width of the pins, though you may find it helpful to draw the dovetails the first couple of times you make the joint.

A dovetail joint made on the bandsaw is simple and fast, and it has a vibrancy lacking in those made with a router jig.

One way to cut dovetails on the bandsaw is to mark them, tilt the bandsaw fence, and simply saw the pins with the fence as a guide.

Cutting Dovetails on a Bandsaw

Bandsaw dovetails have some advantages over dovetails made with a router and jig. First, the setup is less complicated. Second, a mistake in cutting either the pins or the tails doesn't ruin both boards. The layout is easy and doesn't involve much measuring or any drawing. Perhaps most important, dovetails made on a bandsaw don't have the lifeless machine-made quality of dovetails made with a router jig.

Find the dimensions of the spacer blocks

Pin width

Total width of spacer blocks

Number of spacer blocks = number of tails

Stock

1. Determine the width of the pin and subtract that number from the width of the stock. This gives the total width of the spacer blocks. Divide the total width of the spacer blocks by the number of tails in the joint. The result is the width of each spacer block. The number of required spacer blocks equals the number of tails.

Finished joint

Tails

Pins

Tilt the table and set the fence

2. Tilt the table to the right at an angle equal to the dovetail angle. Position the fence to the right of the blade by putting all the spacer blocks between the blade and the fence.

Angle of table = angle of dovetail (typically 8° to 15°)

Fence

Two spacer blocks

Cut the pins

3. Remove one spacer block and cut to the scribed line.

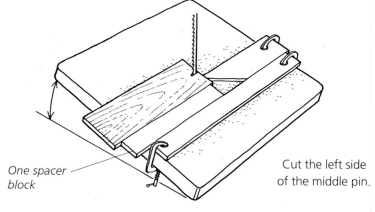

One spacer block

Cut the left side of the middle pin.

4. Remove all the spacer blocks one at a time and make a cut. Make the last cut against the fence.

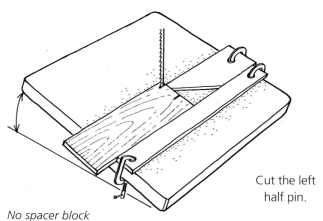

Cut the left half pin.

No spacer block

Tilt the table opposite and repeat

5. Tilt the table in the opposite direction and set the fence to the left. Remove the spacer blocks and make the cuts.

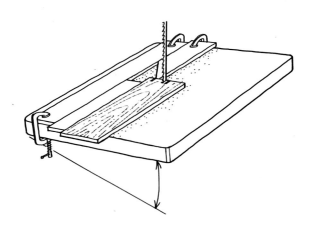

Remove most of the waste between the pins with a bandsaw, but don't try to cut to the baseline. Use a chisel to clean out the waste right along the baseline.

make the spacer blocks by ripping a 2-ft.-long piece of stock to 2⅛ in. wide.

To cut the joint, take a sharp marking gauge and set it for the thickness of the stock, then run it parallel to the ends of the two workpieces. This scribed baseline prevents tearout and keeps the shoulders crisp and clean.

Position the fence by laying the spacer blocks between the fence and the blade, being careful not to bend the blade. Lock the fence and remove one of the blocks. Using the spacer block as the fence, cut the right-hand side of the middle pin. Don't cut right to the scribed line but very near. You might want to use a stop block fastened to the table or the fence to limit the length of the cut, but I typically saw it by eye. Remove the second block and cut the left-hand half pin.

To cut the other side of the dovetail, tilt the table to the left 15° and set the fence using the spacer blocks as before. Again, remove one block and cut the left-hand side of the middle pin, then remove the second block and cut the right-hand half pin. Return the table to 90° and cut out the waste by making a series of parallel cuts that leave each waste area looking like a comb. I don't attempt to saw directly on the scribed baseline. Instead, I use a mallet and a sharp chisel to chop the baseline in the traditional way (see the photo at left).

Once you've completed the pinboard, transfer the layout directly to the tailboard. Do this by positioning the end of the pinboard over the face of the tailboard. Be careful to align the pinboard

Let's assume you're working with a 4¾-in.-wide drawer side. First, you must decide how wide you want your pins to be. This is simply a design decision. I don't think the width of the pins is critical; you can try out various arrangements and see what you like. Let's say the pins will be ½ in. wide. Subtract the pin width from the width of the drawer side to get the total width of the spacer blocks—4¼ in. in this case. Divide by two to get the width of each of two spacer blocks. Next, on the baseline of the tailboard, and then scribe around each pin with an X-Acto knife.

The last step is to saw the tails. You can cut them in the traditional way using a dovetail saw, or you can cut them out freehand on your bandsaw with the table at 90° to the blade. Finally, chisel the waste area between the tails and assemble the joint with gentle taps from a mallet.

If you want to make more than the one full pin and two half pins in this example, simply change the number of spacer blocks. Everything else about the procedure is the same: Decide the pin width, find the total width of the spacer blocks, and divide that by the number of tails you want. The result will be the width of each spacer block. Set up the saw as before, and remove one spacer block to make the first cut. Next, remove each remaining spacer block, make a cut, and continue until you've cut the half pin. Finally, tilt the table the other way, and repeat the steps.

Template Sawing

The fastest way to reproduce identical parts is with a machine guided by a template. Most woodworkers are familiar with the technique as it applies to a router: A bearing, which is fastened to the end of a router bit, runs around the edge of a template fastened to the workpiece. The template is then fastened to the next workpiece, and the process is repeated. All pieces, whether there are 6 or 600, are

Scribe the tails directly from the pins and cut them freehand.

A template and a guide make repetitive cuts fast and easy. All you have to do is feed the stock while making sure it's pressed firmly against the guide.

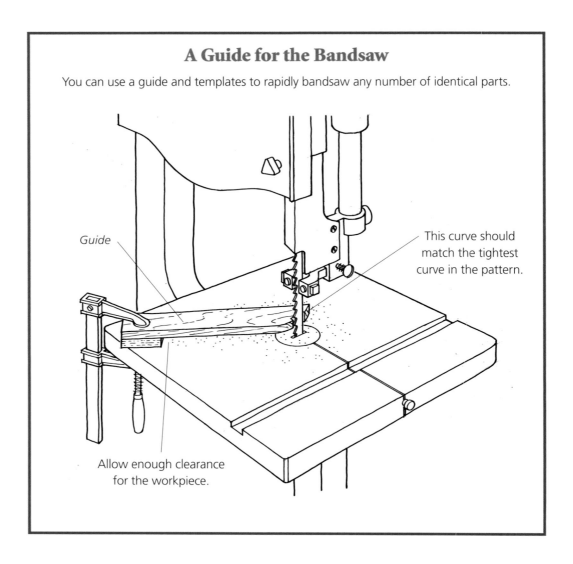

A Guide for the Bandsaw

You can use a guide and templates to rapidly bandsaw any number of identical parts.

Guide

This curve should match the tightest curve in the pattern.

Allow enough clearance for the workpiece.

exact copies because the same template is used to guide the router.

This concept can be applied to a bandsaw for reproducing curves. Rather than drawing the design on the stock and carefully sawing to the line, a template is attached to the stock and the cut is guided by a stick that is secured to the table adjacent to the blade (see the drawing above). This permits you to saw faster because you don't have to concentrate on following the layout line. Instead of following the line, you simply push the stock past the blade while maintaining contact between the template and the guide.

Bandsawing with a template is definitely a fast way to produce any number of curved parts. But the technique does have a major shortcoming: You can't saw inside corners. In fact, the technique is most beneficial for bandsawing large, sweeping curves such as chair rockers.

Also, because making an accurate template may consume a considerable amount of time, the benefit gained by sawing with a template may not outweigh the cost. Nevertheless, bandsawing with a template can be a quick, accurate method for producing large quantities of certain types of work.

For a template, you'll want to use a material that is stiff, strong, and easy to work. I've found that a high-quality plywood is ideal. Inexpensive plywood isn't suitable because it typically isn't flat and it has voids in the core between the veneer layers. Consequently, the guide will catch in the voids and spoil the workpiece.

Making a template is much like making a pattern: You simply draw the design and carefully cut it out. It's also important to sand or otherwise smooth away any irregularities. If you don't take time to smooth away errors, they will be duplicated in any work for which the template is used.

The guide is simply a stick that extends from the blade of the bandsaw to the edge of the table. The business end of the stick, near the blade, is notched to fit around the blade. It's also convex in shape to easily follow the curves of the template. The other end of the stick clamps firmly to the table edge.

With the setup complete, the actual sawing becomes the easiest part of the job. As you're sawing, always keep the template positioned against the guide.

Securing a Template

You can attach a template to your workpiece in a number of ways. My favorite method is to tack the template to the stock with small brads. If you allow the heads to protrude, it's much easier to pull the brads out again. Obviously, you don't want to use brads if the holes will show in the finished work, but typically you can position the brads in an area where they won't be seen or where the offending holes in the stock will later be removed during joinery and construction.

Another option for securing a template to a workpiece is to use double-sided tape. The cloth tape used by woodturners is strong and readily available from many woodworking-supply catalogs. I'm not a fan of this tape because the application is so slow it can often negate any benefits of template sawing.

A third option is to construct a jig that includes the template profile plus toggle clamps to secure the work. Toggle clamps are quick to operate and are ideal for most jig-clamping situations. Because constructing the jig takes time, I reserve this method for parts that I reproduce often.

Make the template a little long

I make the template approximately ½ in. longer than the stock so that the template contacts the guide before the work reaches the blade. This ensures a safe, accurate start to the cut.

Bandsaw Jigs

A well-designed jig can relieve the tedium of laying out and cutting multiple parts, or it can secure an awkward workpiece for safe cutting. In this chapter, I've included a few bandsaw jigs that have worked well for me. Before you begin building, you'll have to adjust the sizes to fit your own bandsaw. With the experience you'll gain with these jigs, I'm sure you'll be able to design your own jig when you're faced with a challenging sawing process.

Stops

The stop is the most common woodworking jig. Stops are used to create a fixed distance for cutting multiple pieces to a specific length or cutting depth. Probably the most common use of a stop when bandsawing is for setting accurate sizes while cutting dovetails or tenons. The stop is simply clamped to the fence behind the blade to limit the length of the cut.

Jigs for Arcs

An arc is a segment of a true circle. Ordinarily you can make an arc by marking a line with a compass and bandsawing to the line. But as you might imagine, this process can be slow and tedious if there's a large number of arcs to cut. To make a jig that cuts an arc, the workpiece must travel past the blade in a curved path. There are two ways of doing this, depending on the size of the work.

Curved fence

The simplest jig for cutting multiple arcs is a curved fence (see the bottom photo on the facing page). The radius of the

A stop can be used to cut multiple pieces to the same length.

This curved fence clamps to the table and guides the workpiece around the blade. It works well for small arcs.

curve in a fence determines the radius of the arc in a workpiece. The first step in making a curved fence is to make a drawing.

Draw a rectangle to represent the workpiece, then draw the arc to be cut on the workpiece (see the drawing on p. 160). Using the same centerpoint as for the arc on the workpiece, extend the leg of the compass until it can draw an arc that contacts the outside corners of the workpiece. Draw in that line—it represents the curve of the fence.

I typically make the fence from plywood. After bandsawing the curve into the fence, smooth the curve with a file or

A Curved Fence for Cutting Small Arcs

Building this arc-cutting fence requires a full-size drawing.

1. Draw a rectangle that represents the workpiece.

2. Using a compass, draw the arc on the near edge of the rectangle.

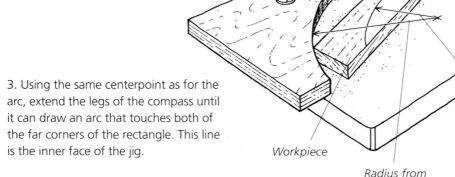

Fence

3. Using the same centerpoint as for the arc, extend the legs of the compass until it can draw an arc that touches both of the far corners of the rectangle. This line is the inner face of the jig.

4. To determine the distance of the fence from the blade, measure the distance between the two arcs on the drawing.

Workpiece

Radius from centerpoint to fence through blade

This measurement determines how far to position the fence from the blade.

a spindle sander. Finally, clamp the fence into position on the bandsaw's table at the distance from the fence to the blade found on the drawing.

Arc jig for large pieces

This jig works well for cutting arcs in large workpieces that may exceed the size of your bandsaw's table (see the photo on the facing page). To use this jig, pivot the arm toward the front of the bandsaw, clamp the workpiece in position, and turn on the power. Next, pivot the arm past the blade.

The jig has two pieces: a base that clamps to your saw's table and a pivoting arm that is mounted to the base. The workpiece is positioned against a stop on the arm and held in place with a stop and a pair of toggle clamps. Then the arm, to which the workpiece is attached, is pivoted past the blade (see the drawing on the facing page).

To build this jig, begin with the base. I use plywood for strength and stiffness. The length of the base must be equal to the radius of the arc plus enough extra length to extend into the throat of your bandsaw so that it can be securely clamped to the table. Cut the width of the base to match the size of your bandsaw's table, then turn the saw on and run the base into position, cutting a kerf. Cut another kerf parallel to the first to make a wide channel that will make it easy to slide the completed jig into position around the blade.

Cut a second piece of plywood for the pivoting arm. The length of the arm should equal the arc radius plus a few extra inches beyond the pivot point to allow room for fastening the pivot bolt. I round the corners of the arm next to the pivot point so I don't knock into them when using the jig. To hold the piece in place, fasten the stop to the arm and

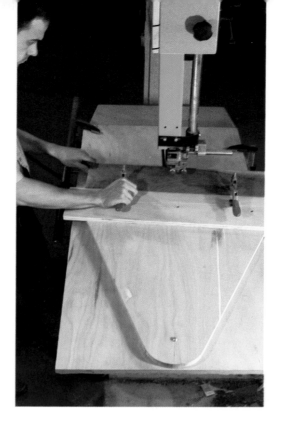

This jig will easily create large, parallel arcs.

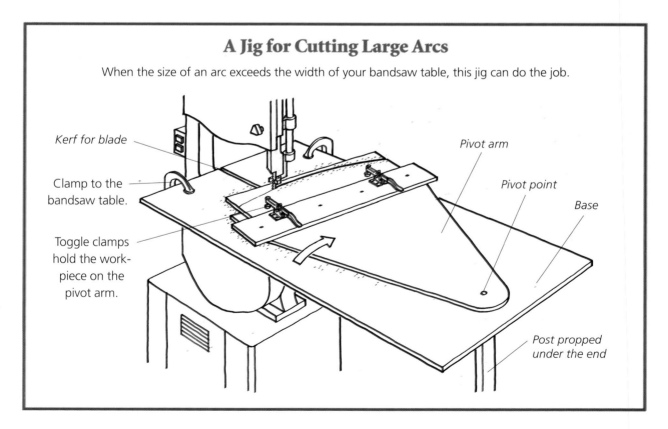

A Jig for Cutting Large Arcs

When the size of an arc exceeds the width of your bandsaw table, this jig can do the job.

Kerf for blade

Clamp to the bandsaw table.

Toggle clamps hold the work-piece on the pivot arm.

Pivot arm

Pivot point

Base

Post propped under the end

mount a pair of toggle clamps. The last step is to fasten the arm to the base at the pivot point.

To use the jig, slide the base around the blade and clamp it to the bandsaw's table. If the jig is large and your bandsaw is small, you may need to attach a length of 2x4 as a leg to support the pivot end of the jig.

Jigs for Circles

Like arc-cutting jigs, a circle-cutting jig guides the workpiece in a path determined by a set radius. The workpiece spins on a pin past the blade to create a circle. The jig consists of a base with a pivot pin that slides in and out to allow you to cut circles of any radius (see the drawing below). You can change the diameter of the circle by changing the distance of the pin to the blade.

Begin by making a plywood base with a wide kerf in one side to accommodate the blade. Next, cut a dovetailed slot for the

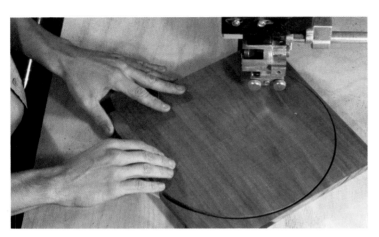

The pivot point of this circle-cutting jig is a pin on the right side of the blade stuck into the underside of the workpiece. The operator rotates the workpiece, and the saw cuts a nearly perfect circle.

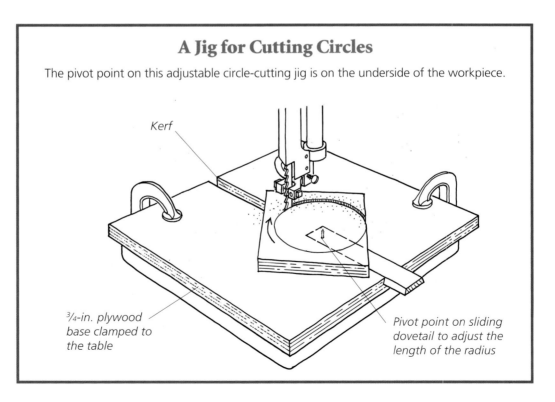

A Jig for Cutting Circles

The pivot point on this adjustable circle-cutting jig is on the underside of the workpiece.

Kerf

³⁄₄-in. plywood base clamped to the table

Pivot point on sliding dovetail to adjust the length of the radius

sliding dovetail that positions the pivot point. Finally, fasten a brad at one end of the sliding dovetail for the pivot point. A screw can be used as a setscrew for locking the pivot point in position.

Fences for Resawing

Resawing a figured plank into veneer requires optimum power and performance from your bandsaw. And the fence is a key component. A good fence should provide rigid support that is absolutely square to the table.

My own bandsaw has a heavy cast-iron fence that is machined flat and locks firmly in position. But if your bandsaw didn't come equipped with a factory-made fence, you can make a suitable fence yourself (see the drawing at right).

The best material for a fence is sheet stock such as medium-density fiberboard (MDF) or a high-quality plywood. The critical part of building this fence is to align the fence wall to the base at absolutely 90°. A pair of triangular braces will strengthen the fence and keep it square.

A high, sturdy fence at right angles to the blade is essential for accurate resawing. Such a fence can easily be made in the shop.

Varnish your jigs for stability

Plywood and MDF are excellent jig-making materials. They are much less likely to warp than solid wood, especially when you coat them with a couple of layers of varnish or cover them with plastic laminate.

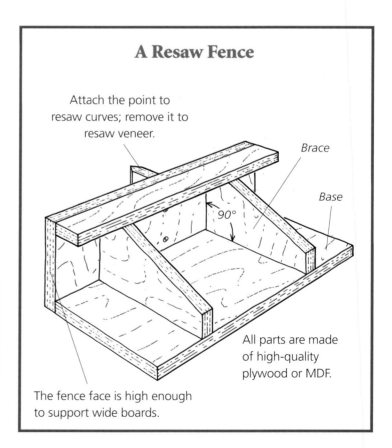

A Resaw Fence

Attach the point to resaw curves; remove it to resaw veneer.

Brace

Base

90°

All parts are made of high-quality plywood or MDF.

The fence face is high enough to support wide boards.

A simple point guide makes it possible to resaw on a curve. It is a long, high pivot point made from a piece of wood chamfered along both sides to a point. It fastens to the resaw fence adjacent to the blade.

Point Guides for Resawing Curves

A point guide is a tall piece of wood chamfered on two sides to make a point all along one side. As simple as it is, it's indispensable for providing support when resawing curves. A point guide also keeps the work at a uniform, consistent thickness.

If you've already made a fence for your bandsaw, then making a point guide is easy. You simply fasten a chamfered stick to your fence with a couple of screws. Once you've finished the bandsawing operation, you can remove the point guide to return the fence to normal use.

Fences for Bandsawing Small Logs

Many of us entered the craft of woodworking because of our love affair with wood. Sure, we enjoy building things, solving cross-grained construction prob-

lems, and using tools, but it's the wood that keeps us coming back for more. What woodworker doesn't thoroughly enjoy seeing the grain pop when the first coat of oil is wiped on?

Although most woodworkers buy their lumber from a nearby lumberyard or perhaps from a mail-order dealer, the most beautiful lumber comes from a log that you saw yourself. That's because the most dramatic grain often comes from areas of a tree that are either considered defects or too troublesome to deal with. For example, loggers normally leave the main fork of a tree in the woods, yet it often has the most dramatic figure in the tree. Other examples include burls, stumpwood, and pieces too short for commercial logging.

But you can saw these "defective" or otherwise undesirable logs on your bandsaw. The key is a coarse, wide blade and a jig for safely guiding the log through the bandsaw. Obviously, you can't saw big logs for large-scale woodworking projects, but depending on the size of your bandsaw, you can saw planks that are suitable for many smaller projects.

When I want to slice a small log into planks, I first build a simple L-shaped jig out of inexpensive plywood (see the drawing on the facing page). I don't bother with high-quality plywood because the jig gets sawn up in use. Build the jig to fit the approximate length and diameter of the log, then fasten the log to the jig with a pair of lag screws. It's important that the screws penetrate the soft bark and bite into the fibrous sapwood.

Some of the most beautiful wood you'll find comes from small logs that were considered too troublesome for commercial loggers. With a simple jig, you can mill these logs into valuable lumber.

The jig runs along the standard band-saw fence to guide the log through the blade in a straight path. For additional support, I sometimes attach a U-shaped channel to the jig that fits over the fence that came with my bandsaw.

When using this setup, I mount a coarse, wide blade, such as one that is 1 in. wide and 1½ pitch, on my bandsaw. Because of the enormous amount of dust produced by this procedure, it's important to use a dust collector with your saw.

You'll need to dry the lumber you've sawn before you can put it to use. I seal the ends of a log with paraffin or a commercial log sealer before slicing it. This limits the amount of damage to the boards from end checking (splits that occur on the ends during drying). Afterwards, I stack the boards and separate the layers with sticks to allow air to circulate around each board. Figure on one year of drying time per inch of thickness.

Depending on the area of the country in which you live, the planks should be dried to a moisture content of 6% to 8%. To achieve this, eventually you'll need to bring the planks into a heated area in your garage or shop for a few weeks before using them.

A Jig for Sawing Small Logs

The jig rides against the standard fence to guide a log through the blade in a series of parallel cuts. The base of the jig is sawn away with each successive cut.

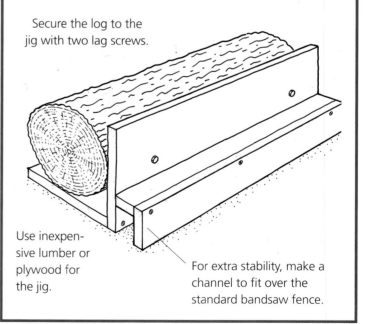

Secure the log to the jig with two lag screws.

Use inexpensive lumber or plywood for the jig.

For extra stability, make a channel to fit over the standard bandsaw fence.

Bandsaw Projects

Learning about the bandsaw is like learning woodworking in general—it's much easier and more fun when you use your new skills on a project. I've provided three projects in this chapter that use the bandsaw as the primary tool. The mitered box is a simple, contemporary-looking project that focuses on resawing skills. The tea table, with its graceful cabriole legs, is a great project for developing skill at cutting contours, especially the compound curves of the legs. The tea caddy, though only a small project, is packed with useful bandsaw techniques from slicing veneer to cutting dovetails.

I've provided detailed drawings of each of the projects and step-by-step guidelines for their construction. The best part is that once you've built these pieces, you'll have gained a whole new set of woodworking skills.

Mitered Box

This box is unique in that the grain matches from corner to corner all the way around the box (see the photo on the facing page). If you've ever tried your hand at making a small box with mitered corners, then you know what a challenge it can be to get the grain to match all the way around. Matching the grain at three of the four corners isn't difficult if you saw the pieces consecutively from one long board (see the drawing on the facing page), but the fourth corner won't match unless you're very lucky. The way to get the grain to match at the fourth corner is to first resaw a thick plank into two thinner ones. By orienting the boards as shown in the drawing on p. 168, you can easily match the grain.

The flowing grain around the outside corners of this mitered box makes it a great showcase for your finest lumber.

Matching the Grain at Three Corners

If you simply cut the pieces for the box consecutively from one long plank, it is difficult to match the grain at every corner.

Lay out the pieces consecutively.

Assemble the pieces this way.

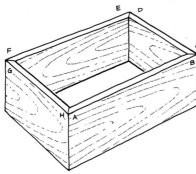

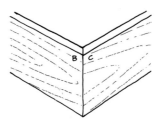

The grain flows around corners B/C, D/E, F/G.

The grain does not match at A/H.

Matching the Grain at All Four Mitered Corners

The key to matching the grain at all four corners of a mitered box is to resaw a board and turn one piece end-for-end before laying out the box.

First book-match, then turn one board end-for-end and lay out the pieces as shown.

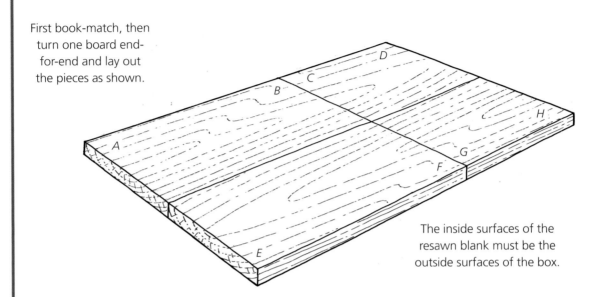

The inside surfaces of the resawn blank must be the outside surfaces of the box.

Assemble the pieces this way.

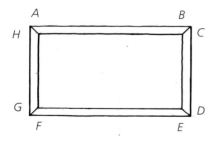

The grain flows around all four corners.

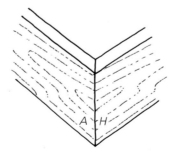
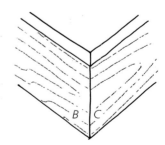

Another neat feature of this box is that the grain matches between the lid and the box. The trick here is to build the box first, then saw the lid free. Although some wood is lost to the kerf, it isn't enough to eliminate the grain match.

Because this box uses the matching corners technique, it's a great way to show off some fantastic figured grain. And because it's small, you won't need a lot of showy lumber. If you're like me, you've got a few small planks stashed away for just this type of project—cutoffs that were too small for use on your last project but just too awesome to throw out.

Begin by flattening one face of the plank with a jointer, then plane it to a thickness that equals the thickness of the box sides plus what you'll lose to the kerf when resawing. This gives a true, flat surface to place against the fence while resawing. Resaw the plank exactly in the middle so that the two boards will be of equal thickness (see the photo at right).

After resawing, remove the bandsaw marks with a razor-sharp handplane. If the wood you're using is highly figured, use a scraper because it will not tear the surface of the wood as a handplane might.

Next, lay the two boards on a bench, and orient the stock to create the effect of the grain flowing continuously around the box. Here's how this works: Each plank must be used for one long side and one short side of the box. The inside surfaces of the resawn plank must be used for the outside surfaces of the box. Place

Resaw the plank for the box into two planks of equal thickness. Clean up the bandsaw marks with a sharp handplane.

Getting the best grain match

To achieve the best grain match, you'll want to resaw with your thinnest blade. The thicker the blade, the wider the kerf and the less likely that the grain in the two planks will match perfectly. I like to use The Wood Slicer from Highland Hardware because its kerf is a mere $\frac{1}{32}$ in.

Mitered Box

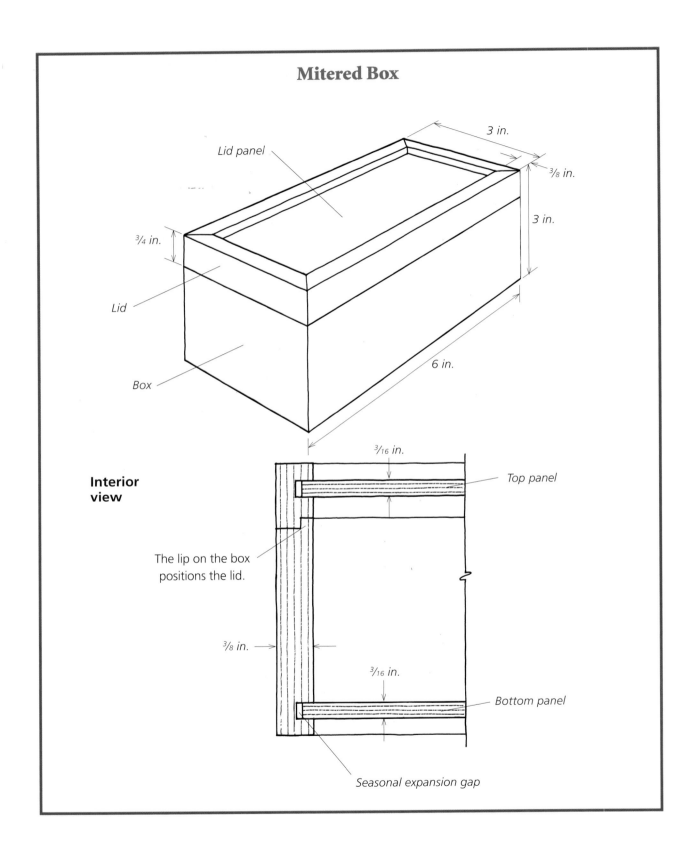

Lid panel

3 in.

3/8 in.

3 in.

3/4 in.

Lid

Box

6 in.

Interior view

3/16 in.

Top panel

The lip on the box positions the lid.

3/8 in.

3/16 in.

Bottom panel

Seasonal expansion gap

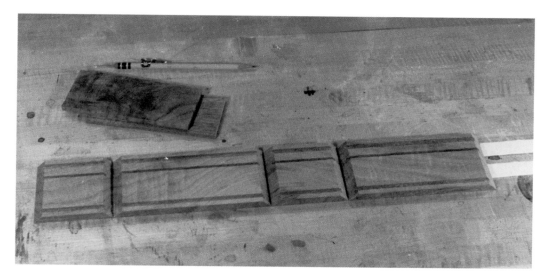

Mitered corners are difficult to clamp. I use masking tape by laying the pieces on the tape and folding the box together.

the two resawn boards edge-to-edge in book-matched fashion, then turn one board end-for-end. You can now picture how the grain will flow from each side of the box to the next.

Cut the grooves for the top and bottom either on a table saw or on a router table, then cut the box sides to length. It's important to cut the parts so that the grain ends on one side and continues on the next. Of course, you'll lose some grain to the kerf, but you can minimize the grain loss and maximize the matching-grain effect by using your thin-kerf bandsaw blade to cut the pieces.

The next step is to miter the ends of the box. To create a precise 45° angle, don't rely on the angle scale on your table saw. Instead, cut four pieces of scrap stock to length and miter them. Then assemble them with masking tape to form a frame, which makes any error in the angle of the blade easy to spot. When you're satisfied with the setup, miter the stock for the box.

Dry-assemble the box and check the fit of the corners. It's nearly impossible to clamp a mitered box because the corners slide and become misaligned, so simply tape the box together. First, lay a length of tape on your workbench with the sticky side up, then position the box sides end-to-end on the tape (see the photo above). Once the four sides are stuck to the tape, simply fold the box together.

While the box is taped together, figure out the dimensions of the top and bottom of the box. When measuring, allow room in the bottom of the groove for seasonal expansion; otherwise, your carefully mitered corners will be pushed apart during humid weather when the wood expands. Do, however, make the thickness of the top and bottom panels a snug fit within their corresponding grooves. This prevents the panels from rattling.

Fine-tuning miters

When checking my test cuts, I look to see if the miters are closed. If the toe of the miter is open, I tilt the blade a tad more. If the heel of the miter is open, I straighten the blade.

Have Fun with the Design

You can have some fun with this box by playing with the design. I purposely made the demonstration box simple to leave you plenty of room to use your imagination. Here are some design suggestions:

- Add contrasting splines to the corners (see the drawing below).

- Add a tiny bead to the top edge of the box where the lid fits (see the top drawing on the facing page).

- Add a tiny chamfer to the box and the lid where they meet (see the top drawing on the facing page).

- Use a raised panel for the lid instead of a flat one (see the bottom drawing on the facing page).

- Carve initials and the date into the lid.

- Inlay a design of contrasting wood into the lid.

- Change the size and proportions to fit something you would like to store in the box.

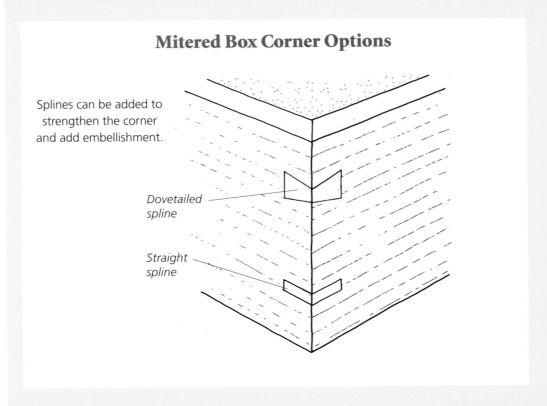

Mitered Box Corner Options

Splines can be added to strengthen the corner and add embellishment.

Dovetailed spline

Straight spline

Mitered Box Lid-Joint Options

Add a tiny bead to the box
with a scratch stock.

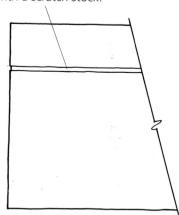

Chamfer the edges of
the lid and box.

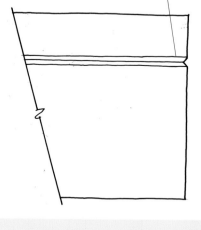

Bandsawn Box Lid Options

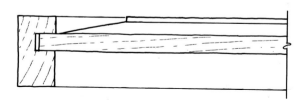

Raised panel

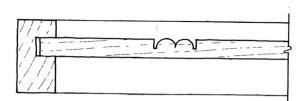

*Double-beaded
flat panel*

Place some glue on the miters and put the top and bottom in place before folding the box together during final assembly.

lid, offset the sawblade slightly from the rabbet you cut earlier on the inside of the box. Complete the box with a final sanding and your favorite finish.

Connecticut Tea Table

Tea was introduced to England from the East during the 17th century. By the 18th century, tea drinking was a popular social custom among the wealthy of both England and colonial America.

As the popularity of tea drinking grew, a market developed for tiny porcelain teacups, silver teapots, tea caddies for storing tea leaves, and delicate, fashionable tables from which to serve the tea. A study of tea tables from the period reveals the remarkable ingenuity of unknown craftsmen.

Compared to other tea tables from the period, this table is simple—but it is definitely not plain. The craftsman who designed this table understood the importance of line and used it to his advantage. The result is a beautiful form that relies on its flowing lines for embellishment rather than heavy, ornate carving. Although the original version of this table was cherry, I made mine from tiger maple because I prefer the distinctive striped figure.

Starting the cabriole legs

When selecting lumber for cabriole legs, choose stock with straight grain that runs parallel to the face of the plank. This avoids having a leg with a weak ankle,

Next, assemble the box by following the same procedure you used when dry-fitting it. Obviously, you'll need to use glue on the miters this time and fit the top and bottom in place as you fold up the box. Once the glue has dried, saw off the lid. I use a table saw and raise the blade just enough to go through one side of the box.

If you don't plan to use hinges, you'll want some method for keeping the lid aligned in place. The technique I use is to cut corresponding rabbets into the box and lid. This is easy to do on a router table after you've cut the lid free from the box. Alternatively, you can cut the rabbet on the inside of the lid before you assemble the box. Afterward, when sawing off the

This tea table relies on flowing lines for embellishment. You will hone your bandsaw skills as you cut the intricate scallops of the skirts and the compound curves in the cabriole legs.

which may later break. Also, it's best to use thick, solid stock for the legs. Cabriole legs made from glued-up stock suffer from distracting glue lines and mismatched color and grain.

First, mill the leg stock to the dimensions given in the drawing on pp. 176-177, allowing 1 in. extra length for the drive center on the lathe. Next, trace the leg outline onto two adjacent surfaces of each blank (see the photo at right). To lay out the mortises in the leg, it's important to trace the pattern back-to-back rather than knee-to-knee.

After tracing the leg pattern, lay out the leg mortises, which accept the tenons on the ends of the rails. I cut the mortises ¾-in. deep with a benchtop hollow-chisel

Trace the outline onto two sides of the stock back-to-back so that you lay out and cut the mortises before bandsawing the piece.

Connecticut Tea Table

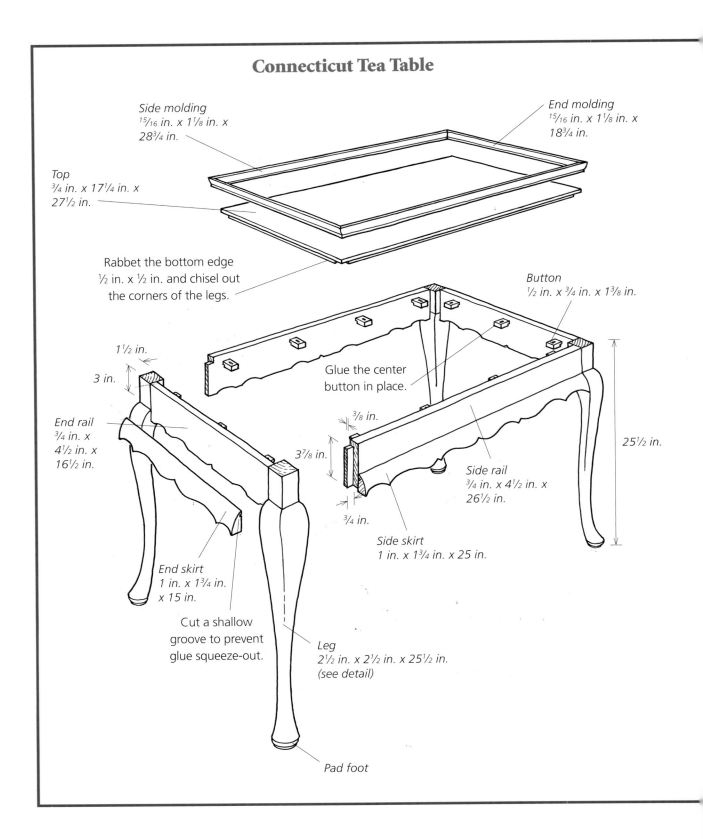

Side molding
$^{15}/_{16}$ in. x $1^1/_8$ in. x $28^3/_4$ in.

End molding
$^{15}/_{16}$ in. x $1^1/_8$ in. x $18^3/_4$ in.

Top
$^3/_4$ in. x $17^1/_4$ in. x $27^1/_2$ in.

Rabbet the bottom edge $^1/_2$ in. x $^1/_2$ in. and chisel out the corners of the legs.

Button
$^1/_2$ in. x $^3/_4$ in. x $1^3/_8$ in.

Glue the center button in place.

$1^1/_2$ in.

3 in.

$^3/_8$ in.

End rail
$^3/_4$ in. x $4^1/_2$ in. x $16^1/_2$ in.

$3^7/_8$ in.

$^3/_4$ in.

$25^1/_2$ in.

Side rail
$^3/_4$ in. x $4^1/_2$ in. x $26^1/_2$ in.

Side skirt
1 in. x $1^3/_4$ in. x 25 in.

End skirt
1 in. x $1^3/_4$ in. x 15 in.

Cut a shallow groove to prevent glue squeeze-out.

Leg
$2^1/_2$ in. x $2^1/_2$ in. x $25^1/_2$ in. (see detail)

Pad foot

Cabriole leg detail

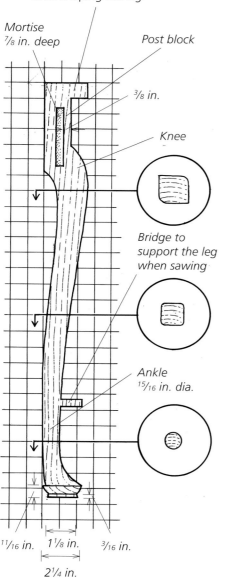

Leave this area full size for the lathe drive center. Cut it off after shaping the leg.

Mortise
7/8 in. deep

Post block

3/8 in.

Knee

Bridge to support the leg when sawing

Ankle
15/16 in. dia.

11/16 in.   1 1/8 in.   3/16 in.

2 1/4 in.

1 square = 1 in.

mortiser, but you could also use your router or even cut them by hand.

Next, bandsaw the contour of the leg. When bandsawing, leave a square bridge to support the leg while cutting the second face (see the top photo on p. 178). Also, leave each end of the leg blank square for the lathe centers. The foot profile must be shaped on a lathe, not on a bandsaw, which is another important reason for leaving this area square. Remember to save the offcut at the back of the leg after sawing the first face. Because the offcut has the drawing of the leg contour, you'll need to tape it back in place for the second cut. After bandsawing the second face, cut off the bridge.

Turning the feet

The foot of the leg is a simple design called a pad foot. Because it is circular, the easiest way to make it is on a lathe. Before mounting the leg, you'll have to locate the turning centers for the foot, which, in this case, are not the centers of the stock. Here is why: The leg stock measures 2 1/2 in. by 2 1/2 in. to accommodate the knee, but the foot is only 2 1/4 in. in diameter. For the leg to look its best, locate the centers on a 2 5/16-in. square; otherwise, the foot will be positioned too far forward. Starting at the

Don't saw the entire leg. Leave the top square to put in the lathe chuck, leave the details of the foot for turning, and leave a bridge to support the piece on the table when making the second cut.

The easiest way to make the foot is to turn it on the lathe. Here, a spindle gouge is used to cut the profile between the foot and pad.

back corner of the leg, measure $2\frac{5}{16}$ in. in each direction. Next, mark diagonal lines across the $2\frac{5}{16}$-in. square. This indicates the true center for turning the foot.

Mount the foot at the tailstock end of the lathe to avoid having your turning tools come in contact with the drive center. Because the leg is asymmetrical, use a slow speed while turning (600 rpm or less), both for safety and to prevent excessive vibration.

Begin by turning the foot round to a diameter of $2\frac{1}{4}$ in. Calipers make it easy to check the accuracy of the diameter and to ensure that all four feet are equal in size. Be careful not to cut into the ankle. Next, mark the top of the foot, and cut a shallow V with a skew. The V creates a distinctive look and a reference point for shaping the leg. Turn the pad to diameter with a parting tool, then turn the foot profile, which starts at the V and ends at the pad. Because the foot is really a bead, roll it over with a $\frac{3}{8}$-in. spindle gouge. Lightly sand the foot and remove it from the lathe.

Shaping the legs

The goal when shaping the legs is to gently round the corners and create smooth, flowing lines. If you were careful to bandsaw closely to the layout lines, shaping each leg is much easier. If not, you'll first have to remove any bumps and irregularities before you begin rounding the corners.

I use a Nicholson #49 rasp to shape the leg. First, secure the leg in a pipe clamp, which should be held in your bench vise. Begin shaping at the front, then move to the back, and finally to the sides, always being conservative by removing wood gradually. You should stop periodically and view the curves of the leg at arm's length to check for flat or dead spots. A chisel works well to blend the curves of the ankle into the V at the top of the foot. Once you've shaped the leg and established the curves, smooth away the rasp marks. I use a file for this step, then I finish up with a scraper.

Making the rails and skirts

Making the rails is a straightforward process. First, mill the stock to the dimensions given in the drawing on p. 176. Cut the tenons for a friction fit within the leg mortises. You can easily cut accurate tenons on your bandsaw if you use a fence and miter gauge to guide the cuts (see pp. 146-149 for details on cutting tenons on the bandsaw). While cutting, make the slots for the 16 buttons that hold the tabletop in place. I make them using a router.

The table shown in the photo on p. 175 is slightly different from the one shown in the drawing on p. 176. The one in the photo has slides on each end for supporting candlesticks, a practical option built into many tea tables in the 18th century. I added them to the table in the photo because I think it is a nice decorative feature that adds detail to the table. If you prefer, you can leave them off. Since many old tables, including the original table I copied, don't have candle slides, your table will still look authentic.

To add the slides, you'll have to cut a slot into the end rail at each end of the table (see the drawing on p. 180). You can

Blend and shape the flowing curves of the leg with a rasp, taking time to make sure the lines are smooth and flowing. Clamp the leg in a pipe clamp, which in turn is held in a bench vise.

The upper part of the leg is shaped with a bandsaw, but below the ankle, the foot is turned. A chisel works well to blend the sawn curves above the ankle into the turned contours of the foot.

Allow room for the top to expand

The tabletop and the buttons will shrink and swell with changes in atmospheric moisture, so you must allow for this when cutting the slots or the table will pull itself apart. The button slots on the sides need about 1/8 in. extra depth on each side. Similarly, the end slots need to be 1/8 in. wider than the buttons to allow side-to-side movement.

Optional Candle Slide Details

Many 18th-century tea tables had slides on each end that pulled out
to provide stands for candles to light the tea service.

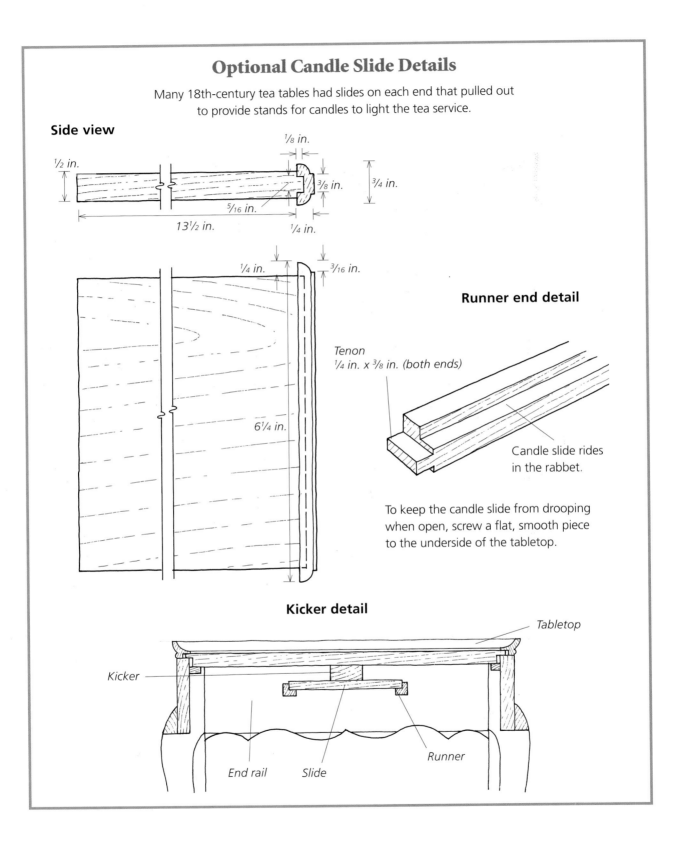

Side view

$\frac{1}{2}$ in.

$\frac{1}{8}$ in.

$\frac{3}{8}$ in.

$\frac{3}{4}$ in.

$\frac{5}{16}$ in.

13$\frac{1}{2}$ in.

$\frac{1}{4}$ in.

$\frac{1}{4}$ in.

$\frac{3}{16}$ in.

6$\frac{1}{4}$ in.

Runner end detail

Tenon
$\frac{1}{4}$ in. x $\frac{3}{8}$ in. (both ends)

Candle slide rides
in the rabbet.

To keep the candle slide from drooping
when open, screw a flat, smooth piece
to the underside of the tabletop.

Kicker detail

Tabletop

Kicker

End rail   Slide

Runner

The first step in gluing the table is to glue one pair of legs to each end rail.

make the slots as a stopped cut on either a table saw or router table. When those are done, make the runners to support the candle slides. These are simply a pair of sticks with a rabbet along one edge to guide and support the slide. I cut tenons on both ends of the runners and mortise them ⅜ in. into the backs of the rails on each end of the table. You'll also need to add a kicker to the underside of the top to keep the slide from drooping when open.

Next, cut the scalloped design into the bottom edge of the rails. This is necessary so that the rail won't be seen behind the skirt. Position the skirt pattern flush with the lower edge of each rail and trace the outline, then use a ¼-in. blade to cut the outline on a bandsaw.

Before making the skirt, glue each end rail to a corresponding pair of legs. Once the glue has dried, use a chisel and block plane to pare the post blocks flush with the surface of the rail.

The faces of the skirts are contoured to match the knees. The best way to match

Match the contours of the skirt to the knees by tracing the knee profile on the ends of the skirt stock.

the contours exactly is by tracing the knee profile onto the ends of the skirt stock (see the photo above). You can create this profile on the skirt using a block plane and scraper, or you can use a shaper. When you're satisfied with the contour on the face of the skirt, you're ready to bandsaw the scalloped outline

One way to shape the skirt profile is to use a block plane and scraper.

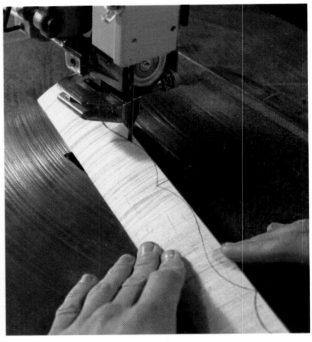

Bandsaw the scalloped outline to the lower edge of the skirts after the profile has been shaped.

Make a template for the skirt profile

If you're shaping the skirt profile by hand, make a thin plywood template of the shape at the knee. You can use it to check the shape of the profile all along its length.

into the lower edge of the skirt (see the right photo above).

The next step is to glue the skirt onto the ends of the table with yellow glue. Because of the skirt's unusual shape, it is difficult to clamp, so I simply press it into place and hold it for three to four minutes until the glue gets tacky. Then I set the assembly aside to allow the glue to fully cure.

Once the glue has dried, blend the curves of the skirt with those of the leg using rasps, files, and a chisel. Beginning with the knee, smooth and blend the surface of the knee to the face of the skirt.

Next, blend the concave area under the knee into the skirt. Once you're satisfied with the contours, smooth the surfaces of the knees. I use a scraper, then sand it lightly with 220-grit sandpaper.

Before gluing together the entire framework of the table, do a dry run to check that each joint member fits and that the joints close tightly. If you've chosen to build candle slides into your table, check the fit of the runners for them. Finally, take diagonal measurements of the table to check for square. Once everything fits together well and square, remove the clamps and apply glue to each mortise wall and tenon face and assemble the table once again. After the glue has dried, add the skirts to the long sides of the table

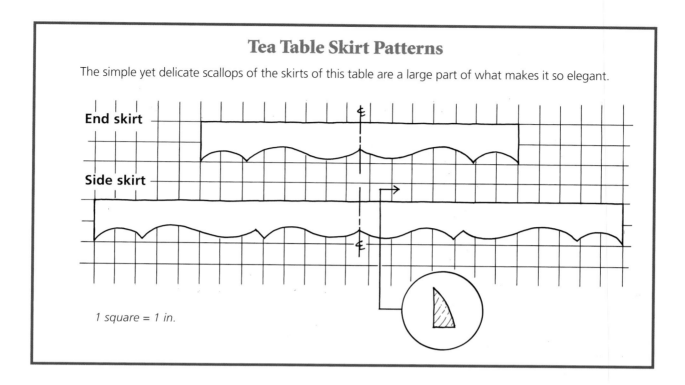

Tea Table Skirt Patterns

The simple yet delicate scallops of the skirts of this table are a large part of what makes it so elegant.

End skirt

Side skirt

1 square = 1 in.

using the same process as was used for the ends.

Making the top

Period furniture is not always built as well as one would like. For instance, on antique tea tables, the top's molding is mitered and nailed directly to the top. This method of cross-grain construction causes the miter joints to pop open, and consequently some old tables are split around the nails. Because of the short-comings of this design, I use a different method of construction to allow for sea-sonal changes in humidity.

I attach the top to the base with wooden buttons, which float within the grooves inside the table rails. Instead of nailing the molding to the top where it

Prefinish the Tea Table

My favorite finish for maple is a honey-colored water-based dye to highlight the curl followed by several coats of shellac. For durability, I'll brush a coat of hard varnish on the top and rub it to an even, low gloss. I finish the table and frame separately, then glue the frame to the table after finishing. This is so that white unfinished edges of the top won't be revealed when the tabletop contracts. It's important to mask the lower edge of the molding and the top edge of the rails during finishing; otherwise, the glue can't penetrate into the wood.

Don't glue the candle slide runners

I don't bother gluing the candle slide runners in place. They add no strength to the table, and once they're in their mortises, they can't come out.

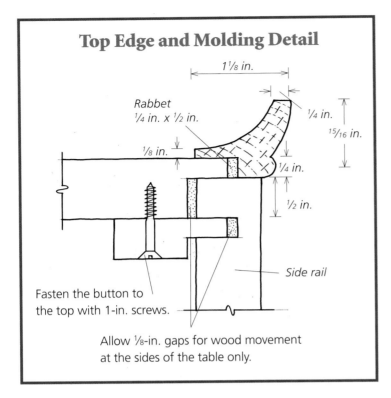

Top Edge and Molding Detail

1⅛ in.

Rabbet
¼ in. x ½ in.

¼ in.

15/16 in.

⅛ in.

¼ in.

½ in.

Side rail

Fasten the button to
the top with 1-in. screws.

Allow ⅛-in. gaps for wood movement
at the sides of the table only.

**Fasten the top of the table to the framework with buttons set
into slots in the backs of the sides and ends. Note the slot and
runner for the candle slide.**

restricts movement, I glue the bottom
edge of the molding to the top edge of the
rails (see the drawing at left). As a result,
the top can float underneath the molding
unrestricted.

I prefer a one-board top on a tea table,
but two wide boards glued together look
fine if you're careful to match the grain.
After milling the top, cut a rabbet around
the perimeter to allow the top to recess
within the table framework. You'll also
have to remove the excess stock under
each corner to let the top sit over the leg-
post blocks. Note that you'll need to cut
the rabbet wide enough to provide room
for top expansion along each edge (see the
drawing at left). Because wood is relatively
stable in length, that isn't necessary at the
ends. Fasten the top to the base assembly
with buttons.

Next, make the molding that runs
around the top edge of the table. I use my
shaper to cut the molding profile, but you
can also use a router table and a scratch
stock (see the drawing on the facing
page). Notice that the molding has a rabbet that fits over the edge of the top. I cut
the rabbet last because the depth of the
rabbet is critical—it must correspond to
the thickness of the top at its edge. Plus,
it's easier and safer to shape the molding
profile on the edge of a wide piece of
stock and rip it free once all the shaping
is completed.

Once the rabbet has been cut, miter the
molding, being sure to check the blade
angle with test pieces as described on
p. 171, then glue it into a frame.

Two Ways to Make the Tabletop Molding

Using a shaper

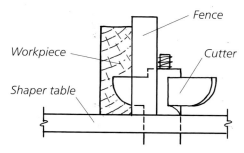

1. Stand the stock on edge and cut the cove first. Because maple is so dense, I made the cut in three passes.

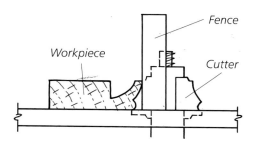

2. Cut the outside edge of the molding.

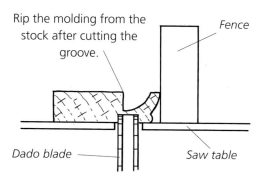

3. Using a dado blade on a table saw, cut a ¼-in.-deep groove on the underside of the molding to fit over the edge of the top, then rip the molding strips from the stock.

Using a router and scratch stock

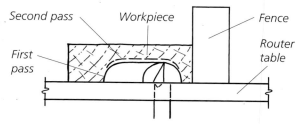

1. Use a 1-in.-dia. core-box bit to waste away the inside edge of the molding. If necessary, clean up the cove with a curved scraper and sandpaper.

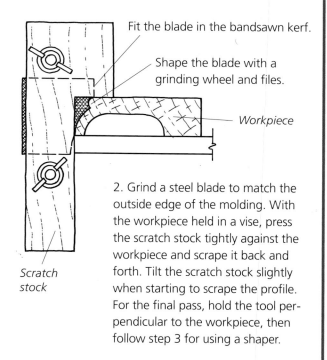

2. Grind a steel blade to match the outside edge of the molding. With the workpiece held in a vise, press the scratch stock tightly against the workpiece and scrape it back and forth. Tilt the scratch stock slightly when starting to scrape the profile. For the final pass, hold the tool perpendicular to the workpiece, then follow step 3 for using a shaper.

When gluing the top to the framework, use a frame made of ¾-in. plywood to distribute the clamping pressure evenly around the table.

The building of this tea caddy makes use of several bandsaw techniques, including resawing, dovetailing, and cutting contours.

Glue the frame in two steps
It's easier to glue a frame in two steps. First, glue a long and a short strip of molding together to form an L. Then glue the two Ls together to complete the frame.

To finish the top, apply glue to the bottom edge of the molding frame and attach it to the top edges of the rails on the table base. I use a ¾-in.-thick plywood frame to evenly distribute clamp pressure all around the top (see the top photo). Be careful to center the frame or the pressure won't be even.

If you opted for candle slides, you can work on them while the glue is drying on the molding. Start by resawing a nicely figured plank and milling the parts to size. The front is a simple molding with a decorative thumbnail profile shaped around the edges. After shaping, cut a stopped groove in the back of the molding to act as a shallow mortise. Next, cut a tenon on one end of each slide to fit snugly within the mortise. After scraping and sanding the parts, glue the front to the slide and attach a small brass pull.

Tea Caddy

This little box is a reproduction of one that was originally used for storage of tea (see the photo at left). Tea and spices were expensive commodities during the 18th century and were typically kept under lock and key. Today, this small chest would make a great little jewelry box or a gift for almost any occasion.

If you are relatively new to woodworking and to the bandsaw, this project will teach you several useful bandsaw techniques. For example, all of the main parts of the box, such as the top, bottom, and sides, are resawn from thicker stock. The box is joined at the corners with dovetails, which you can also cut on your bandsaw.

The Golden Rectangle

Good proportions are vital to the visual success of any piece of furniture, and the small tea caddy is no exception. Some 18th-century cabinetmakers used mathematical systems to achieve pleasing proportions in their furniture.

One such system is called the Golden Rectangle, where the ratio of the shorter side to the longer is 1:1.618. The proportions of the Golden Rectangle are found in many natural objects, and designers, architects,

and craftsmen have used it for centuries. For example, the Parthenon of ancient Greece fits within a Golden Rectangle, as does the modern-day credit card and the front of this tea caddy.

The proportions of the front of the tea caddy match those of the Golden Rectangle, as do the front of the Parthenon and a common credit card.

Tea caddy

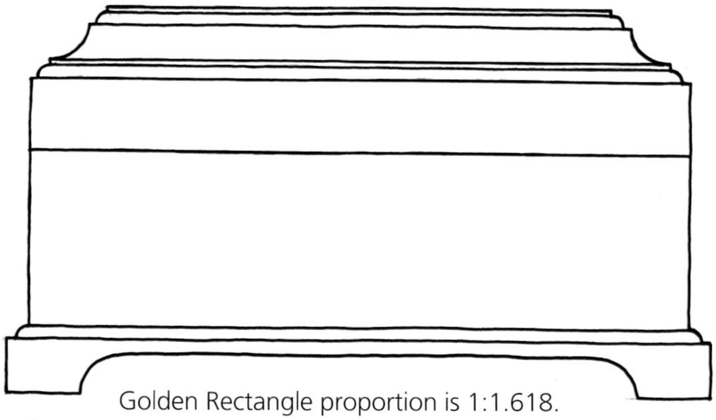

Parthenon

Golden Rectangle proportion is 1:1.618.

The height equals 4 in.
The length to the outside of the box equals 6½ in.

4 x 1.618 = 6.472, round up to 6½ in.

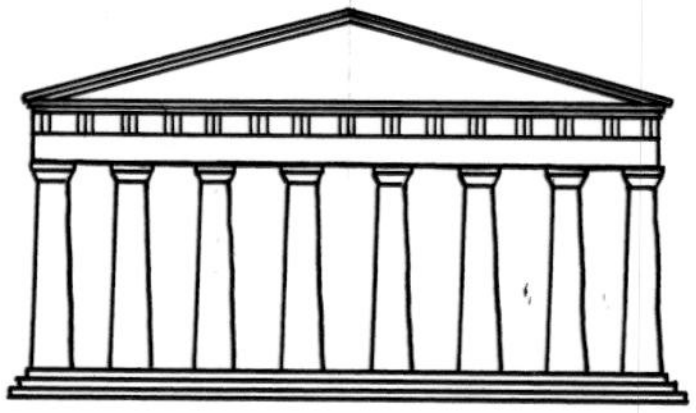

Credit card

ANYBANK USA

0000 2222 3333 4444
123   12/00   √
JOHN Q PUBLIC

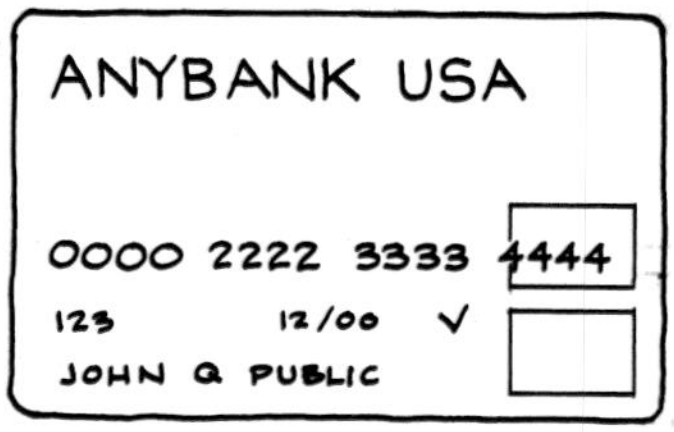

A layer of veneer gives the box a clean, uncluttered look and encourages the viewer to see the simple lines of the box and the figure of the veneer rather than the joinery. Both the veneer and the thin interior partitions can be easily sliced on a bandsaw. Finally, you also use a bandsaw to cut the profiles on the bracket feet.

Tea Caddy

This small project makes use of many bandsaw skills—resawing, cutting contours, and making dovetails.

Top view

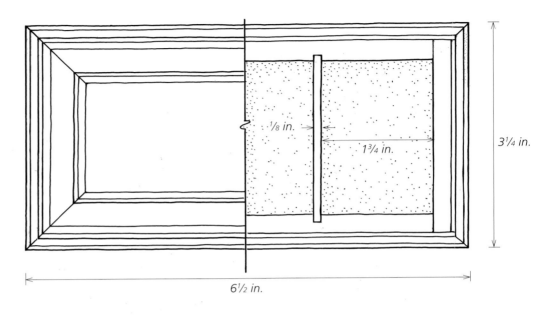

$\frac{1}{8}$ in.

$1\frac{3}{4}$ in.

$3\frac{1}{4}$ in.

$6\frac{1}{2}$ in.

Front view

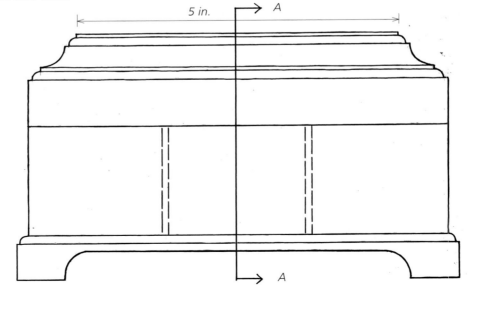

5 in.

A

A

Section A

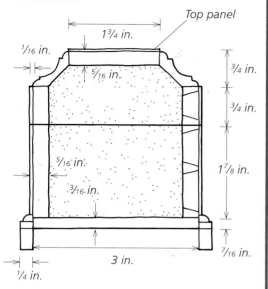

Top panel

1¾ in.

1/16 in.

5/16 in.

¾ in.

¾ in.

5/16 in.

1⅞ in.

3/16 in.

3 in.

7/16 in.

¼ in.

This is a typical dovetail layout. Use a 15°
angle and allow for the joint at the lid.

Lid molding

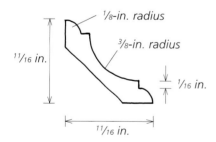

⅛-in. radius

3/8-in. radius

11/16 in.

1/16 in.

11/16 in.

Foot detail

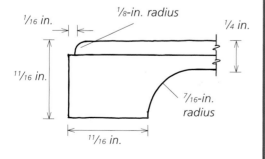

1/16 in.

⅛-in. radius

¼ in.

11/16 in.

7/16-in.
radius

11/16 in.

The box sides and ends are made of walnut and the top and
bottom of quartersawn oak; the outside surfaces are later
veneered to cover the joinery. Resaw these thin parts from
thicker planks on a bandsaw.

Making the substrate

Start this project by resawing the stock for
the box. The front, sides, and back are
made of walnut and later covered with
walnut veneer. For the top and bottom, I
use quartersawn oak, as on the original
tea caddy. Quartersawn oak is dimension-
ally stable, and it doesn't expand enough
during periods of high humidity to push
out the moldings or the feet. Resaw these
parts about 1/16 in. thicker than required,
then plane them to final thickness.

When ripping the box sides and ends
to width, it's important to realize that the
box and lid are cut oversize and made as
one piece. Only after the box is assembled
and veneered is the lid cut free from the
main body of the box. There are two reasons for this. This not only ensures a perfect fit between the box and lid but also

Cut the pins of the box's dovetail joints on a bandsaw.

A laminate trimmer works well for mortising the front piece of the tea caddy for a lock. It can be operated one-handed, and its small base is adequately supported by even a small workpiece.

After milling the box parts, the next step is to lay out and cut the dovetails. Learning to cut perfect dovetails isn't easy, but in this case the veneer will later cover any minor flaws. For more information on how to cut dovetails, see pp. 149-155.

Before assembling the box, you'll have to rout grooves for the inside dividers (if you choose to make them) and a mortise for the lock. I use my router table for creating the divider grooves because it's easy to register the small parts against the fence of a router table. I use a laminate trimmer to cut the mortise for the lock freehand. Its small size is just the thing for such a small workpiece. Next, you're ready to glue together the front, sides, and back to make a box. After the glue has dried, use a handplane to shave the outside surfaces of the box perfectly flush. This is important for creating a flat, uniform surface for the veneer.

Veneering the box

When selecting stock for the veneer, I look for figured planks such as small crotches or pieces of stumpwood. If you can't find a crotch board from your local lumber-yard, you can probably get a small fork from a logger or tree surgeon and slice it into planks on your bandsaw. Of course, if you prefer, you can also use a plank of wood with ordinary grain.

Before slicing the plank into veneer, I smooth and flatten one face using a jointer. This gives me a true, flat surface to register against the bandsaw fence when sawing. If you don't have a jointer or your jointer is too small, you can use a hand-

guarantees that the veneer grain will match perfectly at the joint between the lid and the box. For this to work without making the box slightly shorter, you'll have to mill the box parts to a width that equals the box plus the lid plus ⅛ in. for the kerf of a table-saw blade.

plane instead. I slice the veneer thin, just a tad over the final thickness of ¹⁄₁₆ in. This allows me to sand the bandsaw marks from the face of the veneer.

When arranging the veneer to glue to the box, feel free to be creative and position the veneer in a way that yields the most dramatic effect. When you're satisfied with your arrangement, cut the veneer oversize in both length and width to allow a small amount of overhang for later trimming. Don't forget to veneer one of the quartersawn oak pieces to serve as the top of the box.

Glue the veneer to the ends of the box first so the veneer on the front of the box is uninterrupted by the end grain from the veneer on the box ends. When gluing the veneer, it's important to apply uniform clamp pressure, which evens out the glueline. I use a small block of ¾-in.-thick plywood under the clamp to distribute the pressure evenly.

After the glue has dried, trim the excess veneer flush with the sides of the box on a router table. Don't be tempted to use a block plane for this, or the veneer will likely split. When trimming, move the box over the router bit because that will give you much more control than if you hold the router and move it around the box. Next, glue the veneer to the front and back of the box, then trim the veneer flush on the router table.

I make the box bottom oversize and trim it on the router table with a template-cutting bit after fastening it in place. This is much faster and easier than cutting the bottom to exact size and trying to align

The best veneer comes from wood with dramatic figure. Slice the veneer just over ¹⁄₁₆ in. thick, and remove the bandsaw marks by sanding.

Blades for slicing veneer

Slice the veneer with your best resaw blade for the smoothest possible surface. My favorite resaw blade for this job is a variable-tooth carbide-tipped blade with a 2/3 pitch. If your saw can tension it, go for a 1-in. or wider blade. If you have a 14-in. bandsaw, stick with a ³⁄₈-in.-wide blade.

A scrap of plywood will even out the clamping pressure when gluing on the veneer.

For authenticity, fasten the bottom with small cut nails set flush but not countersunk.

Make the bottom of the box slightly oversize, and trim it flush after it's in place. Use a router table and a template-cutting bit.

Cut the lid from the box

I use a 50-tooth combination blade on a table saw to separate the lid from the box. The blade leaves only a few obscure saw-marks that are easily planed or sanded away. Play it safe by raising the blade only the thickness of the box sides, about ⅜ in.

the edges flush as you nail it. I fasten the bottom with small brads. For authenticity, I use reproduction cut nails, which I drive flush without countersinking (see the top photo at left).

The next step is to cut the lid from the box on a table saw. I start with an end so that the final pass will be on the long side, either the front or the back. At this stage, the lid will be cut free of the box.

If you opted for dividers, this is a good time to fit them in place. Resaw the dividers from thicker stock, and hand-plane them for a snug fit. Then round the top edges of the dividers with a small plane, and slide them into place without glue. Glue isn't necessary to secure the dividers if they fit well. Besides, any squeeze-out of glue would be difficult to remove within the confines of the small interior of the box.

Making the feet

The bracket feet are the next pieces to construct. First, cut the small rabbet into the bottom corners of the box into which the feet are recessed. This detail, which I cut on a router table, creates a neat, clean joint between the feet and the box. The rabbet measures $\frac{1}{16}$ in. by $\frac{1}{4}$ in.; it cuts into the bottom of the box and slightly into the veneer.

Mill the stock for the feet, and shape the ⅛-in. thumbnail profile on the upper edge. The thumbnail breaks the hard, square edge and adds subtle embellishment. Since it also matches the thumbnail in the top molding, it works to visually unify the various elements of the box.

Cut the lid from the box on a table saw, starting with an end so that the last cut will be on one of the sides.

After mitering the feet, trim the contour. The small radius of the curves in the bracket feet requires a narrow ⅛-in. bandsaw blade.

Once these pieces are shaped, miter them to fit around the box.

The foot profile is easy to make on a bandsaw with a ⅛-in.-wide blade. If you use a template and router bit to flush-trim the feet, there's no need to saw right to the line. After the feet are shaped, glue them into the rabbet in the bottom of the box. Put triangular glue blocks into the corners behind each foot to strengthen each miter.

Shaping the molding

The molding on the lid adds distinction to the box and gives it a classic look. It's a simple cove profile flanked by two small thumbnail profiles. I make the molding using my router table (see the photo on p. 194).

Trim the foot contour on a router table with a template and flush-trimming bit. The nail holes won't show because they'll be on the back of the piece.

Make the profile of the box lid molding on a router table, then rip the narrow molding from the wider piece. This photo shows moldings being made on each side of a wider board before being ripped from it.

Because the ⅜-in. cove is the heaviest cut, make it first, then shape the ⅛-in. thumbnail profiles and rip the moldings to size. The last step in creating the molding is to rip the 45° bevel on the back of the molding. Removing this excess is important because it gives the inside of the lid a refined appearance.

Next, miter the molding and fit it to the lid. Notice from the illustration on p. 188 that the molding isn't flush with the edges of the lid. Instead, it is set back 1⁄16 in. to create a small step, called a fillet.

Accurately mitering the molding can be difficult. The miter is a compound angle because of the bevel on the back of the molding. Rather than adjusting my saw to a compound angle, I use a simple jig to support the molding on an angle while it is cut (see the drawing at left).

Making the lid
The tea caddy lid comprises three elements: the main body of the lid (which was sawn earlier from the box), the molding frame, and the veneered top panel. To

---

A Chopsaw Jig for Mitering Small Moldings

This jig rests on the bed of a chopsaw to hold the molding during the cut in the same position it occupies on the finished box. Using this jig is easier than laying the molding flat and trying to cut a compound miter.

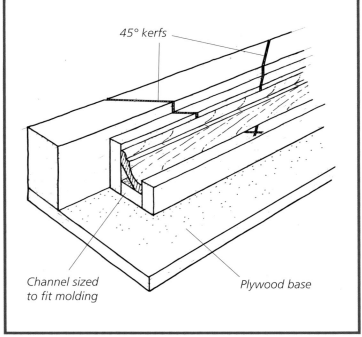

45° kerfs

Channel sized to fit molding

Plywood base

Rip small moldings from wider stock

It's difficult to safely shape such a narrow molding because narrow strips vibrate and are prone to kick back. The safest and most precise way of shaping narrow strips of moldings is to first shape the edges of a wide board, then rip the molding from it (see the photo above). The wide board has mass that dampens vibration and also allows you to position your hands a safe distance from the router bit.

To glue up small moldings, first glue each long and short piece together to form two Ls. Since the Ls are difficult to clamp, use yellow glue and hold the pieces together for three to four minutes until the glue gets tacky. Once the glue has dried completely, glue the two Ls into a frame.

make the lid, begin by gluing the molding segments together at the miter. First, glue each long molding strip to each short strip to form two Ls. When the glue has dried, glue the Ls together to make the rectangular frame, then glue the frame to the lid. I prefer yellow glue for each of these steps because it grabs quickly.

To complete the lid, cut the veneered-oak top panel for a snug fit within the molding frame. The top panel should be cut to exact size and carefully glued within the molding frame. Notice that the top protrudes $\frac{1}{16}$ in. from the frame to create a small fillet that visually becomes part of the molding.

Finishing

The last step in making the tea caddy is to fit the hardware and apply a finish. Before you do, however, notice that the joint between the box and the lid has a tiny quirk bead. Small details like this bead add distinction to your work. It takes only a couple of minutes to create with a scratch stock. After fitting the hardware, remove it and lightly sand all of the surfaces. Finally, finish the box and reinstall the hardware.

That's all there is to it. Not only have you learned several useful bandsaw techniques but you have also made beautiful furniture as well.

Use a stop to set the lengths of mitered pieces

For a precise fit of the molding miters, it is critical that parallel pieces are cut to the exact same length. Even when 45° miters are cut precisely, they will not fit properly to make a frame unless parallel sides are cut to the same length. Measuring, marking, and cutting each piece to precise lengths is slow and difficult, so instead I use a stop attached to a chopsaw jig.

Tea Caddy Hardware

The hardware shown on the tea caddy in the photos is available from Ball & Ball Hardware. Here are the part numbers:
- L105-061 Escutcheon
- E29-903 Pull
- TJB-055 Lock
- H201-001 Hinges

Sources

Bandsaws

Bridgewood
3230 Susquehanna Trail
York, PA 17402-9716
(800) 235-2100
http://www.wilkemach.com

Delta International Machinery
246 Alpha Drive
Pittsburgh, PA 15238
(800) 438-2486
http://www.deltawoodworking.com

Jet Equipment & Tools
P.O. Box 1349
Auburn, WA 98071-1349
(800) 274-6848
http://www.jettools.com

Laguna Tools
2265 Laguna Canyon Road
Laguna Beach, CA 92651
(800) 234-1976
http://www.lagunatools.com

Powermatic
619 Morrison Street
McMinnville, TN 37110
(800) 248-0144
http://www.powermatic.com

Tannewitz, Inc.
0-794 Chicago Drive
Jenison, MI 49428
(800) 458-0590
http://www.tannewitz.com

Bandsaw Blades

Highland Hardware
1045 North Highland Avenue, NE
Atlanta, GA 30306
(800) 241-6748
http://www.highland-hardware.com

Laguna Tools
2265 Laguna Canyon Road
Laguna Beach, CA 92651
(800) 234-1976
http://www.lagunatools.com

Lenox
American Saw & Manufacturing Company
301 Chestnut Street
East Longmeadow, MA 01028
(800) 628-3030
http://www.lenoxsaw.com

The L. S. Starrett Company
121 Crescent Street
Athol, MA 01331
(978) 249-3551
http://www.starrett.com

Suffolk Machinery Corp.
12 Waverly Avenue
Patchogue, NY 11772-1902
(800) 234-7297
http://www.suffolkmachine.com

Blade Tension Meters

Lenox
American Saw & Manufacturing Company
301 Chestnut Street
East Longmeadow, MA 01028
(800) 628-3030
http://www.lenoxsaw.com

The L. S. Starrett Company
121 Crescent Street
Athol, MA 01331
(978) 249-3551
http://www.starrett.com

Dust Collection

Delta International Machinery
246 Alpha Drive
Pittsburgh, PA 15238
(800) 438-2486
http://www.deltawoodworking.com

Oneida Air Systems
1005 West Fayette Street
Syracuse, NY 13204
(315) 476-5151
http://www.oneida-air.com

Guides

Black Diamond Guides
P.O. Box 419
Natick, MA 01760
(508) 653-4480

Carter Products Company, Inc.
437 Spring Street, NE
Grand Rapids, MI 49503
(616) 451-2928
http://www.carterproducts.com

Tannewitz, Inc.
0-794 Chicago Drive
Jenison, MI 49428
(800) 458-0590
http://www.tannewitz.com

Hardware

Ball & Ball Hardware
463 West Lincoln Highway
Exton, PA 19341
(800) 257-3711
http://www.ballandball-us.com

Index

Publisher: Jim Childs

Associate Publisher: Helen Albert

Editors: Aimé Fraser, Jennifer Renjilian

Copy Editor: Diane Sinitsky

Designer: Annemarie Redmond

Layout Artist: Susan Fazekas

Photographer, except where noted: Lonnie Bird

Illustrator: Vince Babak

Indexer: Nancy Bloomer